55 TECHNOLOGY PROJECTS

FOR THE DIGITAL CLASSROOM

Everything you need to integrate computers into K-8 classes

Volume I

2023
V.5

ISBN 978-1-942101-48-2

Printed in the United States of America

What Educators Need to Know to Use This Book

"It's not what the teacher does that's important. It's what the teacher gets the children to do."

Phil Schlecty said that, but it could have been any teacher. Effective education is a classroom culture where students lead in-depth exploration of authentic topics. Two elements make that happen: the integration of technology into learning and the incorporation of projects into lessons--PBL.

Sounds straightforward. Technology plus projects equals learning. It moves learning from a two-dimensional content area into a multidisciplinary setting.

That's worth repeating: By incorporating *computers, software, network-based systems, internet-based programs and research, email* into the classroom, education moves beyond books and lectures in the exploration. The melding of technology and projects fills the holes left when books aren't available, providing equity in scholastic offerings. Students then take responsibility for their schooling—to sleuth out answers to questions that arise in an everyday educational environment that are left behind by a static curriculum. They use higher order thinking which encourages individual accountability and performance-based assessments. It empowers active and experiential learning that is remembered years later. It engages student interest and motivates them to learn. It insists they dig deeper and provides the shovels and trowels to do it. What teacher wouldn't want that?

Project-based learning involves students in making the connections between rigor and relevance, demanding accountability in the classroom.

So, are you sold and now wondering, "Are there guidelines?" Read on.

Aligning to ISTE

Not all states align technology with education standards. Some weave tech into classes; some as a stand-alone.

Luckily, there is a set of standards recognized worldwide as authentic assessments of technology-education integration. These are the National Educational Technology Standards for Students, created by ISTE - the International Society for Technology in Education.

How to Use This Book

Projects included in this book are variously designed for a PC, laptop, Chromebook, or iPad. If you're using a different OS, you'll need to adapt the instructions.

"Leadership is the single most important factor affecting the successful integration of technology. This is true at the state level and at the school level. Schools which have made the most progress are those with energetic and committed leaders." *(from a study on tech integration)*.

You are the leader. If you look help in using technology in the classroom, this book will guide you. Each lesson has been tested over a period of years in K-8 classrooms, fine-tuned to ensure an engaging learning experience that supports authentic questions and open collaboration within an integrated environment.

55 Technology Projects for the Digital Classroom (Volumes I and II) ties each lesson into four areas: 1) higher-order thinking, 2) technology skills addressed, 3) subject area/learning addressed, 3) and ISTE standards covered. See the complete list of skills under 'Skills Taught', and the project list on individual lesson pages. Each skill is covered several times by the time you complete all projects.

Next, the one hundred ten projects in the two volumes are categorized three ways: 1) by subject, 2) by program (software), and 3) by grade level:

Projects by Classroom Subject

This section makes it easy to select the right project for a subject. Each includes:

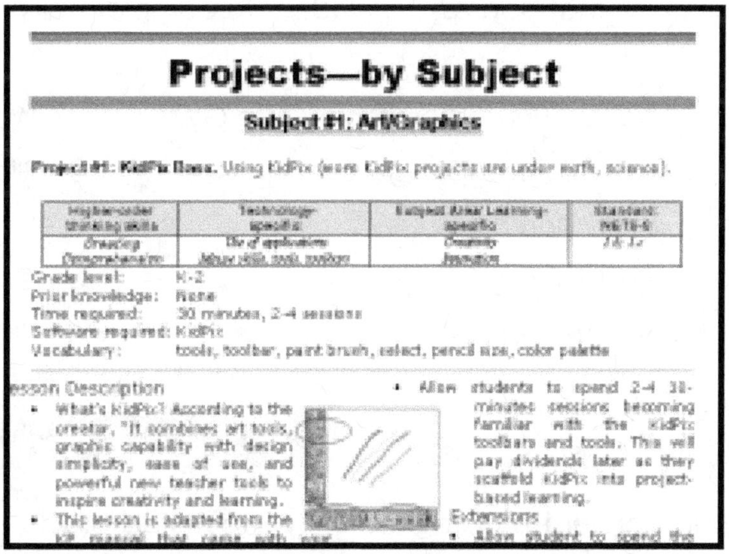

Projects—by Subject

Subject #1: Art/Graphics

Grade level: K-2
Prior knowledge: None
Time required: 30 minutes, 2-4 sessions
Software required: KidPix
Vocabulary: tools, toolbar, paint brush, select, pencil size, color palette

Lesson Description

- What's KidPix? According to the creator, "It combines art tools, graphic capability with design simplicity, ease of use, and powerful new teacher tools to inspire creativity and learning.
- This lesson is adapted from the
- Allow students to spend 2-4 30-minutes sessions becoming familiar with the KidPix toolbars and tools. This will pay dividends later as they scaffold KidPix into project-based learning.

Extensions

- A brief summary of the assignment
- Which grade level it is designed for
- Prior knowledge required, including projects in this series to complete prior to this one
- Time required
- Software required, as well as free alternatives and their download sites.
- Vocabulary required. Use these words in your teaching and require students to use them. By the time you finish 20-30 projects, students will speak geek.
- Higher-order thinking skills addressed
- Technology-specific skills taught
- Core subject supported
- ISTE skills addressed
- Lesson Description—why it's taught and the pedagogy behind it

- Step-by-step lessons. What to teach when so students finish with the least frustration and greatest amount of excitement and discovery.
- Extensions—for deeper exploration
- Troubleshooting tips—from problems I and other technology teachers have experienced in the classroom and how we've solved them
- Examples of projects, including reproducibles for classroom use (grading rubrics, sample projects, checklists, etc.)

Projects by Software

Each lesson is categorized by the software required to complete it. This allows teachers to focus on only the programs available to them. If there's a free version offered on the internet, that address is included. To complete all projects, include:

- *Adobe Photoshop (or the free GIMP)*
- *Celestia and Google Earth*
- *Email and browsers*
- *Art/Drawing*
- *Spreadsheets*
- *Word processing*
- *Slideshows*
- *Desktop Publishing (Publisher)*
- *Oregon Trail (or free online version)*
- *Keyboarding*

Projects by Grade

Each project is categorized by suggested grade level. This determination is made by projects, skills and training that must predate the project, student intellectual maturity, and class time required to instruct students on necessary technical skills. Attention was paid to providing teachers with a selection that fulfills 'typical' state educational standards. For example, there are twenty-one projects that correlate to composition, eleven to geography, ten to language arts, and so on.

Are You a Tech Professional or a Teacher?

There are two ways to use this book:

- As the lab professional, parallel to the core classroom teaching.
- As the teacher interested in integrating technology into your lessons

Either way—same goals, same plans, same pedagogy.

You're a teacher integrating technology into your classroom

You probably use a word processor to create student handouts, a desktop publishing program for the monthly newsletter, email to chat with parents and maybe a spreadsheet to track grades. You might even use the Internet to find cutting-edge lesson ideas. You are what is considered the Web 1.0 teacher—comfortable with technology for your use but struggling to integrate it into the classroom.

But this year, you want to add an active learning component to your lessons that will encourage students to ask authentic questions. You've seen examples of students using technology as part and parcel of the educational process. They're engaged. Learning is student-centered rather than teacher-centered, which means students take responsibility for their own learning, because they've taken ownership. And—here's the scary part—the teacher runs the technology integration into the lesson with assistance from a computer expert

You're the Computer Lab or You're the Integration Specialist

You help teachers find ways to integrate technology into their classroom lessons. You teach computer skills in support of classroom projects in the classroom or technology is a stand-alone class—a 'pull out'—much as Spanish and PE. Use the projects in this book parallel to classroom instruction. What you teach will serve students through high school and beyond, with an emphasis on core software (MS Office, Google Earth, keyboarding, internet, email).

Collaborate with teachers on which projects best support their units of inquiry (i.e., a trifold on colonization to support the fifth grade unit of colonizing). Your job is to be sure students have the skills to complete the project. In kindergarten, you have a year's worth of skills. In fifth grade, you have a vast palette of abilities and programs at your disposal.

Each of the projects in this book can be incorporated by fifth grade. As an integration specialist, I manage about 35 tech projects a year in the nine grades, revolving to keep the program fresh.

Typical 45-minute Lesson

As you face a room full of eager faces, remember that you are a guide, not an autocrat. Use the Socratic Method—don't take over the student's mouse and click for them or type in a web address when they need to learn that skill. Even if it takes longer, guide them to the answer so they aren't afraid of how they got there. If you've been doing this since kindergarten, you know it works. In fact, by the end of kindergarten, you saw remarkable results.

When talking with students, always use the correct vocabulary. That's why I've included it on the lesson plan. Be sure to emphasize the vocabulary and expect students to understand it. Try the Vocabulary Board during one of the quarters/trimesters. Students love it and it highlights why they want to understand 'Geek Speak'.

- Students enter the room. They know to start each class by checking the 'To Do' list on the monitor, taking their seats. You're finishing up the last class but it doesn't matter. Students are responsible for starting the class.

- They start with 10 minutes of typing on the class typing program. Some days, they are directed to work on site words in Spelling City or another activity they can succeed at without teacher direction.
- Next may be one of three presentation activities (*Google Earth Board, Problem-solving Board from Book II in this two-volume series,* or *Vocabulary Board from Book II in this two-volume series*) that rotate throughout the year. Students have selected their topic and presentation date. Whoever is up for the day will teach the class and take questions. This takes 10-12 minutes.
- If it's the beginning of a month, I review assigned homework and take questions. If it's the end of a trimester, I review which skills they accomplished during the last three months.
- If we are starting a new project, I review it with them, take questions and we start. If they are in the middle of one, they use the balance of the class to work towards completion. I monitor activities, answer questions, help where needed.
- During their work, students are free to post vocabulary words they don't understand on the vocabulary board and problem-solving ideas on that board.

- Students who have completed the current project take advantage of 'sponge activities' from a topic of their choice, practice keyboarding for the upcoming speed quiz, or help a classmate struggling with a prickly skill. I include a variety of topical websites on the class internet start page. Students know websites on this page can be used during sponge time.

- Students who finish early may also access the class internet start page. to see what they might have missed in earlier classes.

Skills Taught

The following are critical skills every child should be familiar with and are covered by lessons in this book. Summarized, they include higher-order thinking (adapted from Bloom's Taxonomy of Education Objectives), technology-specific (in text boxes), learning-specific, and ISTE Standards.

Collaboration Skills

- Interact, collaborate and publish with peers, experts or others employing a variety of digital environments and media
- Foster skills important to leadership and group dynamics

- Effectively collaborate, using strong interpersonal skills
- Evoke personal, social, and civic responsibility
- Employ interactive communication
- Produce relevant, high-quality products

Communication skills

- Understand and employ non-linear presentation of ideas
- Effectively use nonlinguistic representations (i.e., graphics, pictures, 3D models)
- Graphically represent problems and solutions
- Communicate ideas multiple audiences using a variety of media and formats
- Write clear, concise letters
- Follow correct protocol for writing paragraphs
- Contribute to teams
- Create bullet lists to explain concepts
- Create outlines to organize ideas
- Exhibit cultural understanding and awareness
- Use graphic organizers to explain ideas
- Use multimedia to explain concepts
- Use visual images instead of words
- Use effective communication, collaboration
- Display effective use of real-world tools
- Produce cogent, pithy, high-quality products
- Use focused methods—multimedia, pictures, diagrams, music, sound, movement, etc., for multi-intelligence communication
- Grammar and Spelling
  - protocols for letter writing
  - tools available to improve work
  - Know how to use tech vocabulary

Email

- *Importance of correct address*
- *Understand body of email (message area)*
- *Paste information into body of email*
- *Use proper netiquette*
- *Use attachments*
- *Use 'to', 'cc', 'subject line'*
- *Check 'sent' file*

Desktop Publishing

- *Identify workspace parts*
- *Understand page layout—colors, shapes, mix of text and pictures*
- *Use templates*
- *Employ an eye for the three c's: color, communication and cohesiveness*
- *Add and delete pages*
- *Add and edit/align text*
- *Add a cover page, Table of Contents, sidebars, pull quotes*
- *Change document view.*
- *Insert, edit, delete frames*
- *Insert and/or change a picture*
- *Preview and print a document*
- *Save, close and reopen a document*
- *Select color and font schemes*
- *Use the Design gallery*

Creativity and Innovation

- Employ creativity in problem solving
- Employ non-linear thinking
- Utilize graphic representation of ideas, problems, solutions
- Apply existing knowledge to new ideas, products and/or processes
- Create original works as a means of personal and/or group expression
- Identify trends and forecast possibilities
- Use models and simulations to explore complex systems and issues

Critical Thinking, Problem Solving, Decision Making

- Produce high-quality products
- Analyze a problem and identify solutions with logic
- Collect and analyze data to identify solutions and/or make informed decisions
- Employ creativity in problem solving
- Don't shy away from curiosity, creativity, risk taking
- Show effective use of real-world tools
- Follow directions
- Use a guided discovery of solutions and learning
- Employ high productivity prioritizing, planning, and managing for best results
- Employ higher order thinking and sound reasoning

Keyboarding

- *Type for speed and accuracy*
- *Correct spacing after a period, question mark, exclamation point, and comma.*
- *Sit up straight, good posture*
- *Center body with elbows at sides*
- *Position feet for balance*
- *Keep hands on home row, curved over keys, wrists off of keyboard*
- *Keep typing project to side of keyboard*
- *Keep eyes on screen or printed copy*
- *Use touch typing, with a smooth rhythm*
- *Know keyboard shortcuts*
- *Stretch fingers*
- *Use correct fingers—usually the one closest to the letter*
- *Use right thumb for spacebar*
- *Use shift key and caps lock correctly*
- *Use right little finger for enter/return*
- *Use left shift to capitalize right hand letters, right shift for left hand letters.*
- *Use right little finger for backspace/delete key*
- *Use left little finger for tab key*

Spreadsheets

- *Use to turn data into information*
- *Analyze data in a problem-solving context*
- *Merge-center cells*
- *Use formulas*
- *Create and format graphs*
- *Create and save workbooks*
- *Enter/sort/format data*
- *Insert hyperlinks*
- *Format cells, columns, rows*
- *Format chart area*
- *Format plot area*
- *Label a chart, axes, legend*
- *Use print-preview to adjust size and layout of document*

- Know how to decode programs you haven't been taught
- Know how to select from various solutions
- Identify and define authentic problems and significant questions for investigation
- Display inventive thinking, adaptability
- Display a bias for non-linear thinking
- Understand options for explaining concepts, reports, information
- Plan and manage activities to develop a solution or complete a project
- Employ self-regulated learning
- Pursue inquiry-based and project-based learning
- Use multiple processes and diverse perspectives to explore alternative solutions

Drawing

- *Add/edit text*
- *Develop eye-hand coordination*
- *Develop mouse skills*
- *Drag-and-drop*
- *Practice fine motor skills*
- *Select the right tool*
- *Understand 'undo'*
- *Understand drawing on the computer*
- *Use fills*
- *Use fonts, font sizes, font colors*
- *Use toolbars*
- *Work with text boxes*

Digital Citizenship

- Produce relevant, high-quality products
- Practice safe, legal and responsible use of information and technology
- Learn about computers and ethics, computers and society
- Demonstrate personal responsibility for lifelong learning
- Exhibit digital citizenship
- Know how to cite work from the internet
- Display personal, social, and civic responsibility
- Understand and employ safe use of the internet

Graphics

- *Resize/crop a picture*
- *Draw geometric shapes*
- *Format a picture*
- *Draw freehand*
- *Move a picture*
- *Use transparencies and recoloring*

Higher-order Thinking (adapted from Bloom's Taxonomy and the Marzano Model for Thinking Skills)

- Analyze:
  - See patterns

- Organize parts
- Recognize hidden meanings
- Identify components

- Apply:
  - Use information
  - Use methods, concepts, theories in new situations
  - Solve problems using required skills or knowledge
- Comprehend:
  - Interpret facts, compare, contrast
  - Order, group, and infer causes
  - Predict consequences
  - Understand information
  - Grasp meaning
  - Translate knowledge into new context
- Evaluate:
  - Assess the value of theories
  - Make choices based on reasoned arguments
  - Verify value of evidence
  - Recognize subjectivity
  - Compare and discriminate between ideas
- Build knowledge
  - Remember dates, events, places, major ideas
  - Observe and recall of information
  - Master subject matter
- Understand:
  - Generalize from given facts
  - Relate knowledge from several areas
  - Predict and draw conclusions
  - Use old ideas to create new ones

Slideshows

- *Add animation-custom animation*
- *Add hyperlinks*
- *Add music to a slide, the entire show*
- *Add pictures*
- *Add slide backgrounds*
- *Add transitions*
- *Add/delete slides*
- *Add/edit/align/format text*
- *Auto-advance slides*
- *Edit pictures, text boxes*
- *Graphically-represent ideas*
- *Navigate from slide-to-slide*
- *Understand slide layout (place savers)*
- *Understand visual learning*
- *Use backgrounds*
- *Use critical thinking skills*
- *Use print preview to print*

Internet

- Know how to find and enter a website address
- Know how to use the browser's toolbar
- Know how to use hyperlinks to maneuver through a website
- Know how to use back-forward buttons, home button
- Know how to add to favorites and use favorites
- Know how to intelligently use the internet for research, how to credit sources, how to pick the most reliable sites, how to refine hits using limiters, extensions and qualified sources
- Know proper internet netiquette
- Know the parts of a web address

Word Processing

- *Edit, format, enter, wrap text*
- *Create original work at keyboard*
- *Use tools and toolbars*
- *Create numbered lists, bullet lists*
- *Find synonyms*
- *Grammar check*
- *Import graphics*
- *Insert borders*
- *Insert, format, resize graphics*
- *Insert headers and footers*
- *Use print-preview before printing*
- *Check page layout (margins, work area, heading-title-body-closing)*
- *Spell-check*
- *Use graphic organizers to explain concepts*
- *Use keyboard shortcuts*
- *Use right-click menus*
- *Change line spacing*
- *Create macros to automate work*
- *Use the cursor to add and edit*
- *Create a table, add/delete rows*
- *Insert watermarks*

Presentation skills

- Know how to prepare and make a class presentation
- Know who your audience is and how to keep the audience interested
- main point is clear
- you have good posture, eye contact, speak with fluency and expression

Research and Information Fluency

- Plan strategies to guide inquiry
- Take surveys and communicate data
- Locate, organize, analyze, evaluate, synthesize and ethically use information from a variety of sources and media
- Evaluate and select information sources and digital tools based on the appropriateness to specific tasks
- Process data and report results

Technology Operations and Concepts

- Create wallpaper using a drawing program or pictures from a file folder
- Understand and use technology systems
- Select and use applications effectively and productively
- Troubleshoot systems and applications
- Transfer current knowledge to learning of new technologies
- Copy from-paste to
- Know correct use of equipment, computer etiquette
- Drag-and-drop data/info between programs
- Close a program
- Be able to use print preview, print and save
- Make wallpaper for desktop
- Use mouse skills
- Know how parts of a computer connect
- Understand right-click menus
- Know the difference between save and save-as
- Know how to save to external drive
- Understand technology vocabulary
- Know how to turn computer/monitor on
- Use a program you haven't been taught
- Use flash drives and other external drives
- Use icons to open a program
- Use scroll bars to maneuver through a page
- Use Task Manager to shut down a program or the computer
- Use caps lock key
- Use shift key to capitalize a letter
- Use clock to find the date
- Use taskbar, toolbars, menu bars
- Use Word Pad, Notepad

Google Earth

- *Copy locations to another file under 'My Places'*
- *Create a tour*
- *Find latitudes and longitudes*
- *Fly-to a location*
- *Mark locations*
- *Measure distances*
- *Save images to 'My Places'*
- *Save locations under 'My Places' to another location*
- *Use Google Earth Community*

Image Editing

- *Understand 'Actions' tool*
- *Understand 'History' layer*
- *Add frames*
- *Add text*
- *Employ auto fixes*
- *Understand when to use which clone tool*
- *Employ different cropping tools for different uses*
- *Format pictures*
- *Use artistic renderings*
- *Use History, Art brush*
- *Use paint brushes*

TABLE OF CONTENTS

Projects—by Subject

Click on the Subject to go to that section; then, scroll down to your desired project

Projects—by Program

Projects—by Grade

Kindergarten-Second grade

Google Earth
- Project 38: Introduction to Google Earth
- Project 42: Where Did I Come From?

Internet
- Project 35: Sponge Activities for Vocabulary
- Project 48: Sponge Activities for Geography
- Project 54: Sponge Activities in History

Keyboarding
- Project 55: Keyboarding in the Classroom

KidPix
- Project 1: KidPix Basx
- Project 2: KidPix Basx II
- Project 3: I Can Make My Own Wallpaper
- Project 13: Art Online
- Project 14: Sponge Activities for Drawing
- Project 20: A Holiday Card—in KidPix
- Project 25: Four-sentence Story
- Project 34: What's a Dolch Word
- Project 42: Where Did I Come From?

MS Excel
- Project 12: Creating Simple Shapes with Excel

First-Second grade

Google Earth
- Project 38: Introduction to Google Earth
- Project 42: Where Did I Come From? (KidPix, Google Earth)

Internet
- Project 13: Art Online
- Project 14: Sponge Activities for Drawing and Graphics
- Project 35: Sponge Activities for Vocabulary
- Project 48: Sponge Activities for Geography
- Project 54: Sponge Activities in History

Keyboarding
- Project 55: Keyboarding in the Classroom

KidPix
- Project 1: KidPix Basx
- Project 2: KidPix Basx II
- Project 3: I Can Make My Own Wallpaper
- Project 13: Art Online
- Project 14: Sponge Activities for Graphics
- Project 16: A Holiday Memory
- Project 19: My Bookcover (in KidPix)
- Project 20: A Holiday Card—in KidPix
- Project 25: Four-sentence Story in KidPix
- Project 34: What's a Dolch Word
- Project 35: Sponge Activities for Vocabulary
- Project 42: Where Did I Come From?

MS Excel
- Project 12: Creating Shapes with Excel

Second-Fourth grade

Google Earth
- Project 38: Introduction to Google Earth
- Project 42: Where Did I Come From?

Internet
- Project 13: Art Online
- Project 14: Sponge Activities for Drawing
- Project 35: Sponge Activities for Vocab
- Project 48: Sponge Activities for Geography
- Project 54: Sponge Activities in History

Keyboarding
- Project 55: Keyboarding in the Classroom

KidPix
- Project 1: KidPix Basx
- Project 2: KidPix Basx II
- Project 3: I Can Make My Own Wallpaper
- Project 16: A Holiday Memory
- Project 18: Holiday Greetings
- Project 19: My Bookcover
- Project 20: A Holiday Card—in KidPix
- Project 26: Four-sentence Story—II
- Project 32: Color My Grammar (in MS Word)
- Project 34: What's a Dolch Word
- Project 42: Where Did I Come From?
- Project 43: Color My World (with KidPix)
- Project 44: What's 'NWSE'? (in KidPix)

MS Excel
- Project 12: Creating Shapes —Excel. PP
- Project 26: Four-sentence Story—II

MS Publisher
- Project 21: A Holiday Card in Publisher
- Project 22: A Holiday Flier in Publisher

MS Word
- Project 15: A Holiday Letter in Word
- Project 16: A Holiday Memory
- Project 17: A Holiday Story in Word
- Project 18: Holiday Greetings
- Project 33: Grow Your Story using Word

Third-Sixth grade

Google Earth
- Project 38: Introduction to Google Earth
- Project 39: Google Earth Board
- Project 41: Where is That? (Google Earth)

Internet
- Project 13: Art Online
- Project 14: Sponge Activities for Graphics
- Project 27: Online Blogs
- Project 35: Sponge Activities for Vocabulary
- Project 48: Sponge Activities for Geography
- Project 54: Sponge Activities in History

Keyboarding
- Project 55: Keyboarding in the Classroom

MS Excel
- Project 12: Creating Simple Shapes—Excel

MS PowerPoint
- Project 29: All About Me—in PowerPoint
- Project 47: Tour the World

MS Publisher
- Project 21: A Holiday Card in Publisher
- Project 22: A Holiday Flier in Publisher
- Project 23: A Holiday Calendar in Publisher
- Project 28: My Storybook—in Publisher
- Project 30: A Cover Page in Publisher
- Project 31: A Title Page
- Project 52: Indigenous Cultures Magazine

MS Word
- Project 15: A Holiday Letter in Word
- Project 16: A Holiday Memory
- Project 17: A Holiday Story in Word
- Project 18: Holiday Greetings in Word, KidPix
- Project 30: A Cover Page in Publisher
- Project 31: A Title Page in Word
- Project 32: Color My Grammar (in Word)
- Project 37: Oregon Trail
- Project 45: Where Am I (with MS Word)
- Project 46: Landforms Table in Word

Technology Basx
- Project 27: Online Blogs

Fourth-Seventh grade

Google Earth
- Project 39: Google Earth Board
- Project 41: Where is That? (Google Earth)

Internet
- Project 13: Art Online
- Project 14: Sponge Activities for Graphics
- Project 35: Sponge Activities for Vocabulary
- Project 48: Sponge Activities for Geography
- Project 54: Sponge Activities in History

Keyboarding
- Project 55: Keyboarding in the Classroom

MS Excel
- Project 12: Creating Shapes with Excel

MS Publisher
- Project 22: A Holiday Flier in Publisher
- Project 23: A Holiday Calendar in Publisher
- Project 28: My Storybook—in Publisher
- Project 30: A Cover Page in Publisher
- Project 31: A Title Page in Word
- Project 49: California Missions Magazine
- Project 51: This Day in History/ in My Life

MS Word
- Project 4: Divide and Conquer
- Project 15: A Holiday Letter in Word
- Project 17: A Holiday Story in Word
- Project 31: A Title Page in Word

Project 32: Color My Grammar (in Word)
Project 33: Grow Your Story Using Word
Project 47: Ecosystems Outline in Word

Oregon Trail
Project 37: Oregon Trail

Technology Basx
Project 3: I Can Make My Own Wallpaper

Fifth-Eighth grade

Google Earth
Project 39: Google Earth Board
Project 40: The Wonders of Google Earth
Project 41: Where is That? (Google Earth)

Internet
Project 13: Art Online
Project 14: Sponge Activities for Drawing
Project 27: Online Blogs
Project 35: Sponge Activities for Vocabulary
Project 37: Class Blog
Project 48: Sponge Activities for Geography
Project 54: Sponge Activities in History

Keyboarding
Project 55: Keyboarding in the Classroom

MS PowerPoint
Project 47: Tour the World

MS Publisher
Project 21: A Holiday Card in Publisher
Project 22: A Holiday Flier in Publisher
Project 23: A Holiday Calendar in Publisher
Project 24: A Holiday Newsletter in Publisher
Project 28: My Storybook
Project 30: A Cover Page in Publisher
Project 31: A Title Page
Project 50: American Revolution Magazine
Project 53: A Colonization Brochure

MS Word
Project 4: Divide and Conquer—Graphics
Project 15: A Holiday Letter I Word
Project 17: A Holiday Story in Word
Project 30: A Cover Page in Publisher
Project 31: A Title Page in Word
Project 32: Color My Grammar (in Word)
Project 33: Grow Your Story Using Word

Photoshop
Project 3: I Can Make My Own Wallpaper
Project 5: Photoshop Basx
Project 6: Quick Fixes in Photoshop
Project 7: Cropping in Photoshop
Project 8: Cloning in Photoshop
Project 9: Artistic Rendering in Photoshop
Project 10: Drawing in Photoshop
Project 11: Photoshop Actions; History Brush

Technology Basx
Project 4: I Can Make My Own Wallpaper

Projects—by Subject

Subject #1: Art/Graphics

Project #1: KidPix Basx I. Students learn tools, toolbars, drag-drop, multi-media, menus—tech basics applied to any drawing/art program

Higher-order thinking skills	Technology-specific:	Subject Area/ Learning-specific	Standard: ISTE
Creating *Comprehension*	*Use of applications* *Mouse skills, tools, toolbars*	*Creativity* *Innovation*	*4a-b*

Grade level: K-3
Prior knowledge: None
Time required: 30 minutes, 1-2 sessions (take your time)
Software required: KidPix (or adapt for another drawing program)
Vocabulary: tools, toolbar, paint brush, select, drag-and-drop, color palette

Lesson Description

- According to the creator, "KidPix combines art tools, graphic capability, ease of use, and powerful teacher tools to inspire creativity and learning."
- This lesson hones mouse skills and introduces the use of tools and toolbars.

Computer Activity

Note: This can be adapted to a variety of digital drawing tools.

- Have students open KidPix. Discuss the program. Discuss how drawing on the computer is different from paper.
- Select the pencil tool on the left side. Try all four associated tools (pencil, chalk, crayon, magic marker) at the bottom, as well as the shapes (filled and unfilled). Try different colors on the palette.
- Repeat with the paint brush.
- Skip the microphone, spray can and wacky tool for now.
- Have students spend 2-4 30-minute sessions becoming familiar with the KidPix pencil and paint brushes. You want them comfortable and confident enough to scaffold KidPix into project-based learning.

Extensions

- Students can spend the extra minutes at the end of class trying other tools of their choice—the paint bucket, spray can, stamps stickers—whatever catches their attention.

Troubleshooting Tips

- *I can't find the tool. (KidPix has many toolbars. Are you on the pencil/paint brush on the left side? Which tool is selected at the bottom? What about selections in the middle of the lower toolbar. So many choices, but that's what makes this classic children's drawing program so robust.)*

As students learn to draw digitally, they perfect mouse skills—drag-and-drop, left click, how to hold the mouse. Here are a few reminders that will help them develop good mouse habits as early as Kindergarten:

MOUSE CONTROL

Single Click:

Select

Double Click:

Open

Right Click:

Choices—Drop-down menu

Websites to Teach K/1 Mouse Skills

Kindergartners get confused about right and left mouse buttons. Why wouldn't they? They've barely learned what those terms mean. I found an easy way to clarify:

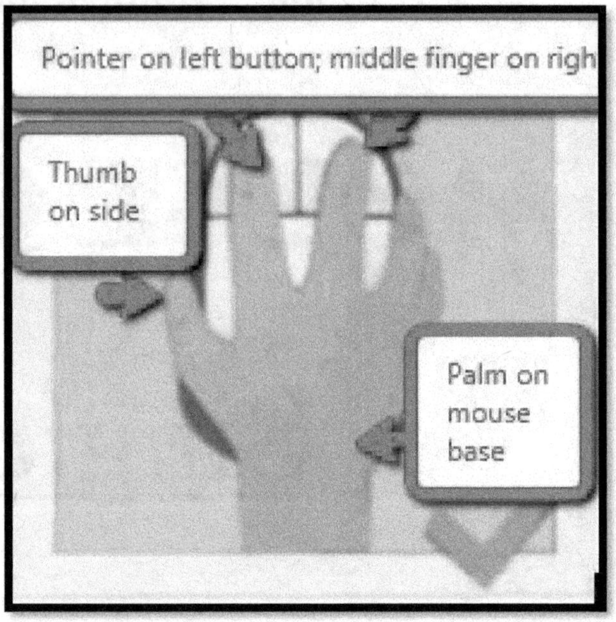

ME: *"Right click with your mouse"*

STUDENT: *Student promptly clicks with their left mouse. I know–doesn't make sense. It does to them. They're happy to focus on the right hand and have no idea they need to go one level further.*

ME: *"The other right."*

Here are mouse websites to teach kindergartners and first graders how to use the mouse:

1. Bees and Honey
2. Drawing Melody
3. Mouse practice w/ the piano
4. Mouse practice
5. Mouse skills
6. Mouse Song
7. OwlieBoo–mouse practice
8. Wack-a-gopher (no gophers hurt)

Kids love puzzles and they're great for practicing mouse skills. Try these:

1. Digipuzzles
2. Jigsaw Planet
3. Jigsaw puzzles
4. Jigzone–puzzles
5. Jigsaw Puzzles

Subject #1: Art/Graphics

Project #2: KidPix Basx II. Use KidPix or any digital coloring pages—a familiar concept for every child, to learn more about tools, toolbars, mouse skills.

Higher-order thinking skills	Technology-specific:	Subject Area/ Learning-specific	Standard: ISTE
Creating *Comprehension*	*Use of applications* *Mouse skills, tools, toolbars*	*Creativity* *Innovation*	*4a-b*

Grade level: K-2
Prior knowledge: KidPix Basx I
Time required: 30 minutes, 2 sessions
Software required: KidPix (or adapt for other drawing programs)
Vocabulary: Palette, bucket, fill, background, tools, toolbar, scroll

Lesson Description,

- According to the creator, "KidPix combines art tools, graphic capability with ease of use and powerful new teacher tools to inspire creativity and learning."
- This lesson simulates a coloring book, providing a great variety of fills with the paint can tool.

Computer Activity

Note: This can be adapted to a variety of digital drawing tools.

- Open KidPix. Select the background tool (looks like trees/grass) on the left side of screen. Go to the toolbar at the bottom and select the 'Color Me' menu. Scroll through the choices at the bottom and drag-and-drop the one you like.
- Select the paint bucket on left. Notice the three buckets that appear at the bottom, next to the textures. Create three different pictures, one with each paint bucket.
- First: Select a color from the color palette, paint bucket #1 and a texture from the bottom toolbar (scroll through the pages of options). Click the mouse to pour between the lines of the design (see top drawing on next page). Change the texture for each segment of the coloring page.
- 2nd/3rd grade: Ignore the color palette. Switch between textures. (see bottom drawing on next page)
- Have older students print without help. Save to student folder; save-as to flash drive.

Extensions

- Students cans spend the extra time at the end of class trying out other tools of their choice—the dog animations, the spray can, stamps stickers—whatever catches their attention.

Troubleshooting Tips

- *I can't find the tool. (Be sure to select the left tool before the bottom tool.)*
- *I don't like the fill I used (Click on the Oops Guy. Do it right away—he only goes back one step.)*

Drawing with #1 paint bucket and one color:

Drawing with #3 paint bucket (fills)

Subject #1: Art/Graphics

Project #3: I Can Make My Own Wallpaper Kids love to personalize the computer stations. Show them how to create their own wallpaper using internet pictures, pictures on the computer or their own drawings

Higher-order thinking skills	Technology-specific:	Subject Area/ Learning-specific	Standard: ISTE
Creating, understanding	*Drawing skills, Windows skills, KidPix basics*	*Art, critical thinking, creative thinking*	*4a-b*

Grade level: 2-6
Prior knowledge: Project 1 and 2: KidPix Basx I/II, Project 5: Photoshop Basx, Windows Basics
Time required: 20-30 minutes (for drawing and installing)
Software required: KidPix (or another art/drawing app)
Vocabulary: wallpaper, .jpg, .gif, .tif, export, drill down, browse, right-click

Lesson Description

- According to the creator, "KidPix combines art tools, graphic capability with ease of use to inspire creativity and learning." KidPix is the original drawing software, easy enough for the youngest artist. Older children will want to use Photoshop or Gimp.
- This project appeals to a student's desire for personal, quick and easy with an outstanding result.

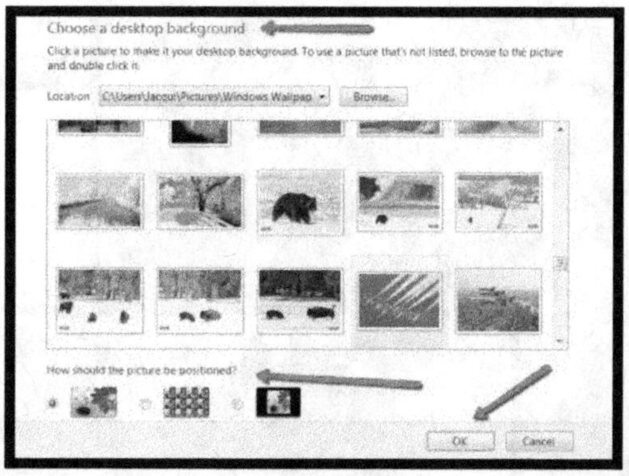

Computer Activity

- KidPix: Draw a picture (see samples on next page). Export (Don't 'Save' because most programs can't read the file extension used for KidPix) to 'My Pictures'.
- Photoshop: Use the skills learned in Projects 9 and 10 to draw a picture. Save it to 'My Pictures' as a .bmp, .jpg, or .tif.
- Right click on the desktop. Select 'Personalize—Desktop background'.
- Browse for the picture you saved in 'My Pictures' and select. Under 'Position', select 'fit to screen'.
- Say 'OK'

Extensions

- Use a favorite photo for wallpaper.
- Show students how to browse to other locations for other pictures.
- For more skilled learners, wallpaper can also be made in Paint (free with Windows), Photoshop or other drawing program. Save as a .jpg, .gif, .tif, .bmp or any other graphic file.

Troubleshooting Tips

- *I can't find 'My Pictures'. (When you export or save, browse for where you saved; drill down)*
- *How do I get photos into 'My Pictures? (It's probably the default 'save' location, but digital cameras allow you to select where you save.)*

Wallpaper made with drawing programs:

Subject #1: Art/Graphics

Project #4: Divide and Conquer. Teach basic photo-editing skills (borders, backgrounds, transparencies, fills, rotate, cropping) available in MS Word (or adapted to other word processing programs). Great for school projects and to introduce Photoshop, GIMP or other advanced photo editing programs.

Higher-order thinking skills	Technology-specific:	Subject Area/ Learning-specific	Standard: ISTE
Evaluating, assess knowledge, observe, recall	*Graphics basics (resize, crop, background)*	*Creativity and Innovation (non-linear thinking, original works)*	*4b, 6a*

Grade level: 4-7
Prior knowledge: Intermediate-level Word or word processing skills
Time required: 45 minutes
Software required: MS Word or similar word processing program
Vocabulary: crop, resize, transparency, background, fill, wrap, watermark

Lesson Description

- Use a picture with several images to learn MS Word photo editing tools like cropping, borders, fill, rotating, resizing.
- The skills presented here are the most common for editing photos and pictures.
- Once mastered, students will be prepared to learn the more-advanced Photoshop editing skills.

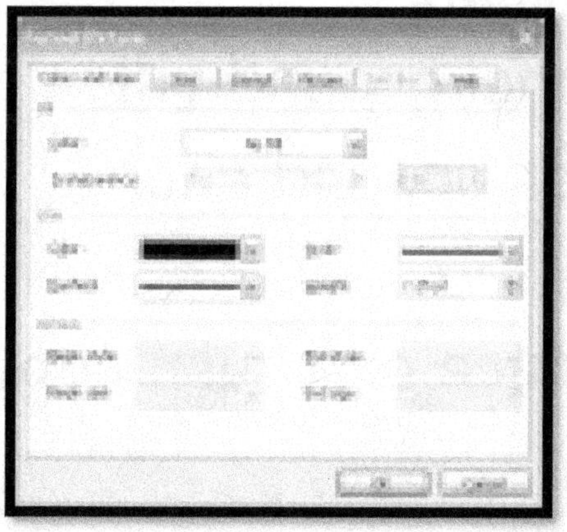

Computer Activity

- Open a blank document in MS Word. Insert a picture with multiple focal points (see samples below).
- Duplicate the image once for each focal point.

- Click one image to activate ribbon toolbar.

Crop each duplicate to show just one of the focal points (see next page)

- Try as many tools on the ribbon as you'd like. For example, change the fill and border. Change the background to washout, grayscale, etc. Change the 'picture style' and Shape. When you're done, say OK.
- Click image once to display the 'dot. Rotate picture creatively.
- If you use pictures from the internet, be sure they're royalty free.

Extensions

- Change the picture's wrap (Format Picture dialogue box) so text flows around the image (tight or square). Resize with handles.

Troubleshooting Tips

- *I can't find the Picture Toolbar (Right-click in the toolbar area of the screen. Select 'Picture' from list)*

PICTURE MANIPULATION

Note: Adapt these steps to your word processing program. Skip those that don't work.

1. Crop each person
2. Change the background fill
3. Place a border around each picture
4. Copy the picture and turn copy into watermark
5. Rotate
6. Wrap words around, square, behind
7. Put a dog in the picture, in front of the little girl
8. Make dog's background transparent with the pen tool on the picture tool bar

Subject #1: Art/Graphics

Project #5: Photoshop Basx. This lesson introduces the Photoshop layout. Students review the basic tools, choose a picture, use tools and layers to alter the picture

Higher-order thinking skills	Technology-specific:	Subject Area/ Learning-specific	Standard: ISTE
Applying information, creating knowledge	*photo editing*	*Communication skills, creativity and innovation*	*4a-d, 6a*

Grade level: 5-8
Prior knowledge: Project 4 (graphics in Word),
Time required: 45 minutes, 1-2 sessions
Software required: Adobe Photoshop (or adapt for another photo editing tool)
Vocabulary: photo editing, graphics, default, toolbar, layers, history, how to's, pixels, workspace, toggle

Lesson Description

- Adobe Photoshop is KidPix for grownups—and the default photo enthusiasts.
- This project introduces a traditionally-challenging program in a classroom-tested easy to understand set of steps and projects. To avoid the frustration and confusion inherent in most Photoshop training, start with this project before attempting others.

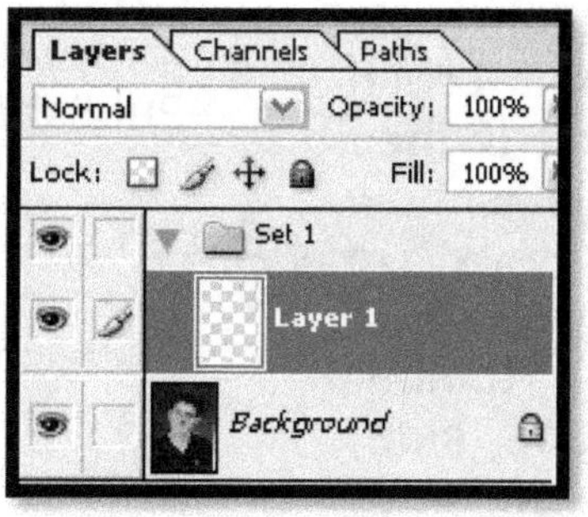

- Students become active, engaged learners as each skill dynamically builds from prior knowledge, and positive learning outcomes spark enthusiasm for more.

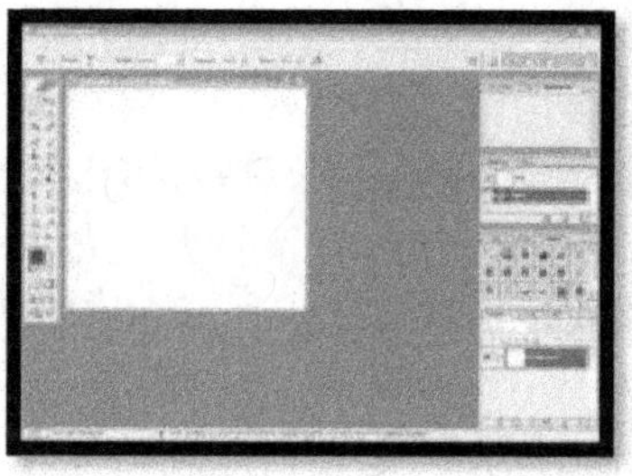

- Demonstrate each skill first, using a smart board or a monitor, and then walk around to be sure students understand.

Computer Activity

Note: If you don't use Adobe Photoshop in your school, adapt this lesson to your preferred image editing digital tool.

- Open Photoshop. Explain the screen layout and toolbars (sides, top and bottom). Briefly describe the right-hand tools (briefly because this book won't get into most of them).
- Click the File Browser tool. It exposes folders and documents on the local computer. Select a picture and notice how it displays all data—file name, size, date created, author, copyright and more.

- Review the menu bar at the top with its choices. Go to Help. Have students view several of the 'How To' wizards available. Make sure they try 'How to paint and draw', 'How to print photos', 'How to save for other applications'. Then have them select the 'Help' files. This takes them to the Adobe CS website and exposes a vast database of questions and answers. Encourage them to explore, engage their critical thinking and active learning skills. Remind them this is where they can find answers independent of teacher assistance.

- Open student school picture. Show class how to zoom in and out (right-side toolbar). Explain pixels. Show them how they can take the paint brush and color just one pixel if they are close enough. This is how experts remove 'red eye' in photos.
- Introduce the History toolbar (right side) as an undo feature (like Ctrl+Z in Word). Have students open a new blank canvas. Notice the size, the background color. Name it. Now draw on it. Use the history tool to toggle between the canvas before and after drawing on it by clicking between the original picture and the last action taken (at the bottom of the History list).

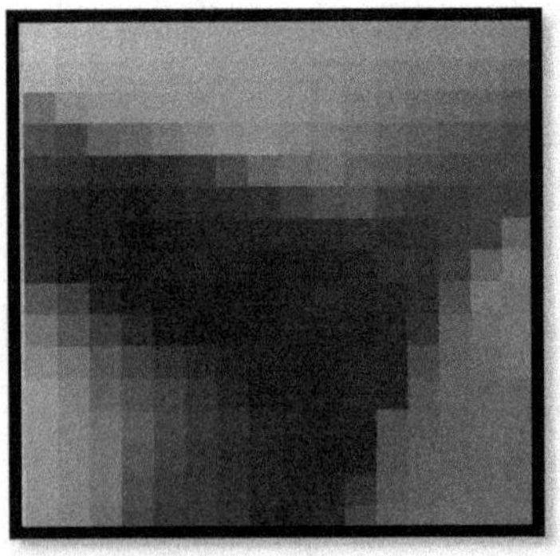

- Have students click through several tools  on the left tool bar and show them how the top toolbar 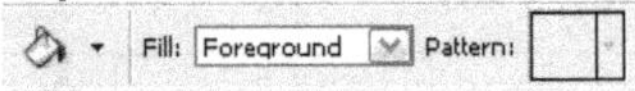 changes, depending upon the tool selected.

- Watch the layers tools. You can only paint on the highlighted layer. Notice that the top layer covers all others

- Show students how to save. The default is as a Photoshop file with a .psd extension. This won't open in other programs, so show students how to change the file type format to a .jpg, .bmp, .tif or other for use in Word, Publisher, emails or a website.

Extensions
- Search YouTube for how-to videos on Photoshop. There are many. Watch several.
- There is also an endless supply of websites that teach Photoshop for beginners, as well as how to perform specific functions (such as ridding a photo of the red eye mentioned earlier).

Troubleshooting Tips
- *I closed some of the toolbars by accident. What do I do? (Go to the menu bar. Select 'Window-workspace-default workspace.)*
- *I can't draw on the picture I opened. (Check that you've selected the paint or pencil tool, that you're not trying to paint with the color white, and that you've selected the correct layer.)*

Subject #1: Art/Graphics

Project #6: Quick Fixes in Photoshop. Learn three quick and easy auto-correct tools to change photos from amateur to pro. Have kids bring their own pictures or select pictures they would like to use. They learn auto-correction.

Higher-order thinking skills	Technology-specific:	Subject Area/ Learning-specific	Standard: ISTE
Applying information, creating knowledge	*photo editing*	*Communication skills, creativity and innovation*	*4a-d; 6a*

Grade level: 5-8
Prior knowledge: Project 5 (Photoshop Basx)
Time required: 20 minutes
Software required: Adobe Photoshop (or adapt for your class photo editing app)
Vocabulary: image, auto, toggle, history,

Lesson Description

- Adobe Photoshop is the grown-up KidPix. If you Google 'Photoshop', you get 179 million enthusiastic hits. For photographers and graphic artists, there is no substitute.
- If you haven't taught Project 5, start there to provide Photoshop basics. There's no friendly cursor, list of templates or prompts to get you started. Photoshop users instinctively know what to do and don't want to waste time on clues.
- Demonstrate first, and then walk around to be sure students can find each tool

Computer Activity

Note: If you don't use Adobe Photoshop in your school, adapt this lesson to your preferred image editing digital tool.

- Have students open a picture from a file folder you've set up of 'Photoshop Pictures'. Pre-test photos to find one that is most representative of these auto-fixes. Some are not as obvious when changed.
- Go to image-adjustments; use the three auto corrections:
    - auto levels

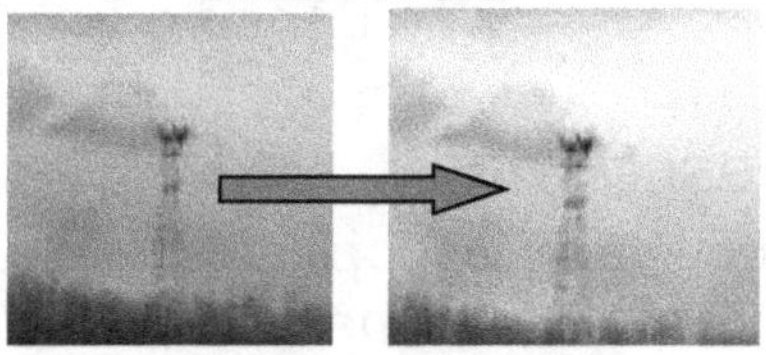

    - auto contrast

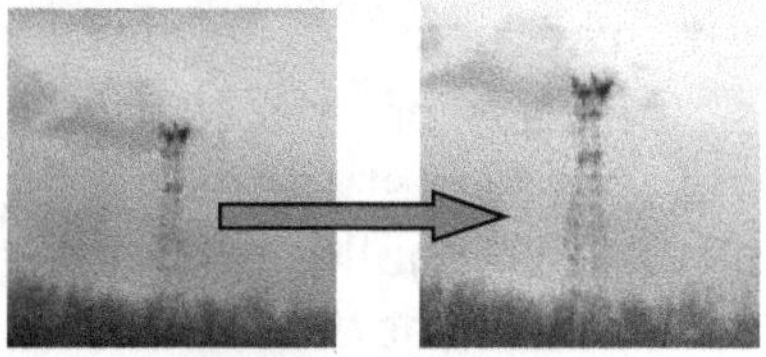

    - auto color

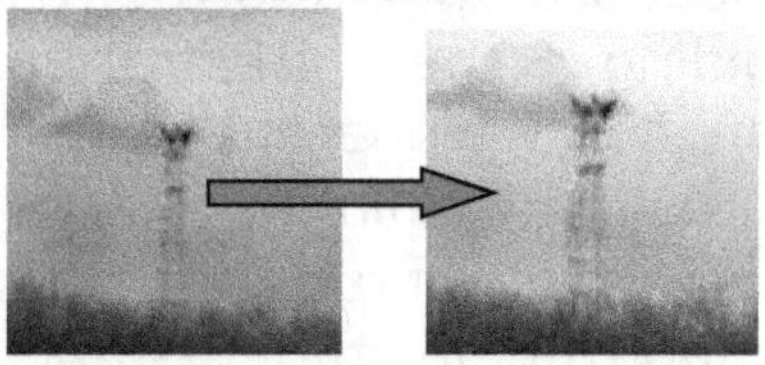

- Do them one at a time and notice the difference.

Extensions

- Go to the 'History' tab on the right. Toggle between the original picture and the corrected picture. Can you see the difference?

Troubleshooting Tips

- *I don't see any difference. (You won't see a huge difference all the time.)*

Subject #1: Art/Graphics

Project #7: Cropping in Photoshop. Learn three ways to crop pictures in Photoshop—lasso, marquis, magic wand—and when to select each. Have students use pictures for a class project or one of themselves—or even one that collaborates with writing skills or language arts.

Higher-order thinking skills	Technology-specific: Photoshop	Subject Area/ Learning-specific	Standard: ISTE
Applying information, creating knowledge	*photo editing*	*Communication skills, creativity and innovation*	*4a, 4b, 4d, 6a*

Grade level: 5-8
Prior knowledge: Project 4 (Graphics in Word), Project 5 (Photoshop Basx)
Time required: 45 minutes
Software required: Photoshop (or your class photo editing tool)
Vocabulary: crop, lasso, magic wand, menu bar, toolbar, background, icon, dancing ants, transform, scale, copy-paste, drag-drop, inverse

Lesson Description

- Adobe Photoshop is the grown-up KidPix, and the default photo-editing program for anyone serious about graphics.
- This series of projects (#5-11) introduces students to a traditionally-challenging program in an easy to understand way, each project scaffolding to the next, thus avoiding the frustration and confusion inherent in most Photoshop training.
- Demonstrate first, and then walk around to help students find tools.

Computer Activity

Note: If you don't use Adobe Photoshop in your school, adapt this lesson to your preferred image editing digital tool.

- There are three ways to crop in Photoshop (remind students of MS Word's single method)

- #1: The crop tool  on left toolbar is best for cutting out a square from a larger picture. Have students open a picture with a uniform background (like the iguana set against the sky on the next page) and cut a square around its head (see sample on next page).
- #2: The lasso tool  on the left toolbar. This one works for any situation. It requires patience and time, but it'll get the job done. Enlarge picture so the area you are working on fills the screen. Click to start lasso; work as carefully as possible. End back where you started. Select inverse to select the background (not the picture). Push delete to remove the background. You should now have the residual image.
- #3: The magic wand tool . This one is the easiest, but only works when there is consistency of color in the background you want to delete. Select the

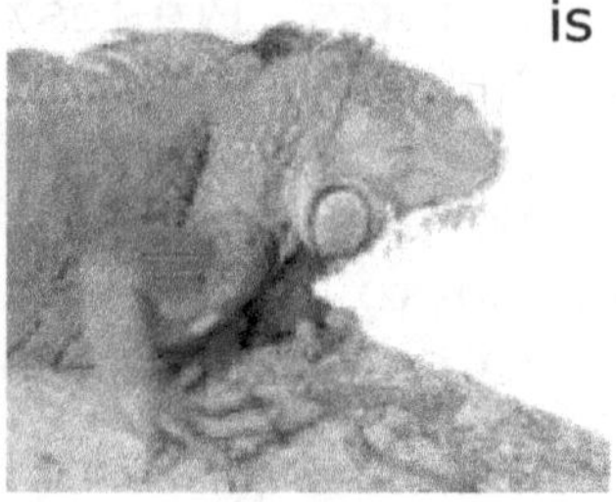

magic wand from the left toolbar. Before beginning, check the toolbar that accompanies the magic wand, at the top. 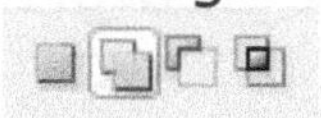 Show students how to select 'add-to' or 'delete from' selection, depending upon which icon they highlight. Have them select 'add-to'. Now click where you want to delete. Continue selecting until all unnecessary background is removed.

- Regardless of the cropping method you selected, now select-inverse on the menu bar at the top. That moves the dancing ants to your selection rather than the deleted background.
- You are ready to save or copy to another picture.

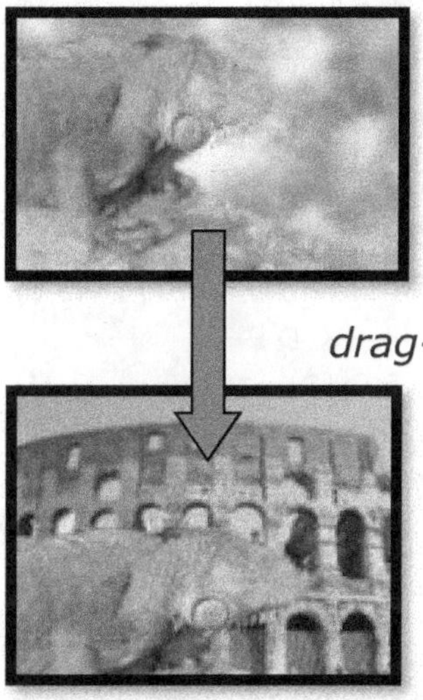

- Open a second picture of a background (i.e., the Coliseum in the sample) without closing the first.
- Copy-paste or drag-drop picture into the new background.
- Use edit-transform-scale to resize picture to suit the new background
- Add several of the pictures to the same background, to create a herd
- Try a different background. Some work better than others.

Troubleshooting Tips

- *When I copy-paste or drag-drop my adjusted picture to its new background, all I get is an empty shape (Did you select inverse first?)*
- *I'm trying to drag the picture but I get an error message (Do you have the correct layer highlighted?)*

Extensions

Here are completed Photoshop projects:

Subject #1: Art/Graphics

Project #8: Cloning in Photoshop. Add or subtract features from a picture (i.e., flowers); clone from one picture to another. This can be used to create a picture for a classroom unit of inquiry, or to teach about ethical issues (because cloning looks authentic)

Higher-order thinking skills	Technology-specific:	Subject Area/ Learning-specific	Standard: ISTE
Applying information, creating knowledge	*photo editing,*	*Communication skills, creativity and innovation*	*4a, 4d, 6b, 6d*

Grade level: 5-8
Prior knowledge: Project 5 (Photoshop Basx)
Time required: 45 minutes
Software required: Adobe Photoshop (or your class photo editing tool)
Vocabulary: clone, anchor point, CTRL click, click,

Lesson Description

- Adobe Photoshop is the default photo-editing program for serious graphics artists.
- These projects (#5-11) introduce a challenging program in an easy to understand way, avoiding the frustration usually part of Photoshop training.
- Demonstrate and then walk around to be sure students can find tools.

Computer Activity

Note: If you don't use Photoshop, adapt this lesson to a preferred image editing tool.

- The clone tool duplicates a hard to crop-and-copy image (like the flowers) or deletes part of a background—a sign or a post in a nature scene.
- You can clone within a picture (as with the flowers), or from one picture to another (see next page—adding polar bears to the sea cave).
- To duplicate part of a picture (in the case of the flowers), select the clone tool and create an anchor point on a flower with CTRL Click. Now paint with the mouse where you want to clone it (see second picture below).
- To delete part of a picture (such as the flowers), set the anchor point on the green field. Click on a flower and paint over it with the green field until the flowers melt into the background. Be sure to pay attention to shadows, obstructions, etc., so the deletion appears seamless.

Extensions

- Enlarge one bloom by cloning additional petals around the stamen

Troubleshooting Tips

- *It doesn't look right. (check your starting point. Does it match the color and shade of the end point? Have you picked up any extras in the clone process?)*
- *I'm trying to drag the picture but I get an error message (Check your layers. Do you have the correct layer highlighted?)*

Start with an image you like. Select a background you'd like your image to move into. Clone the original image into its new location.

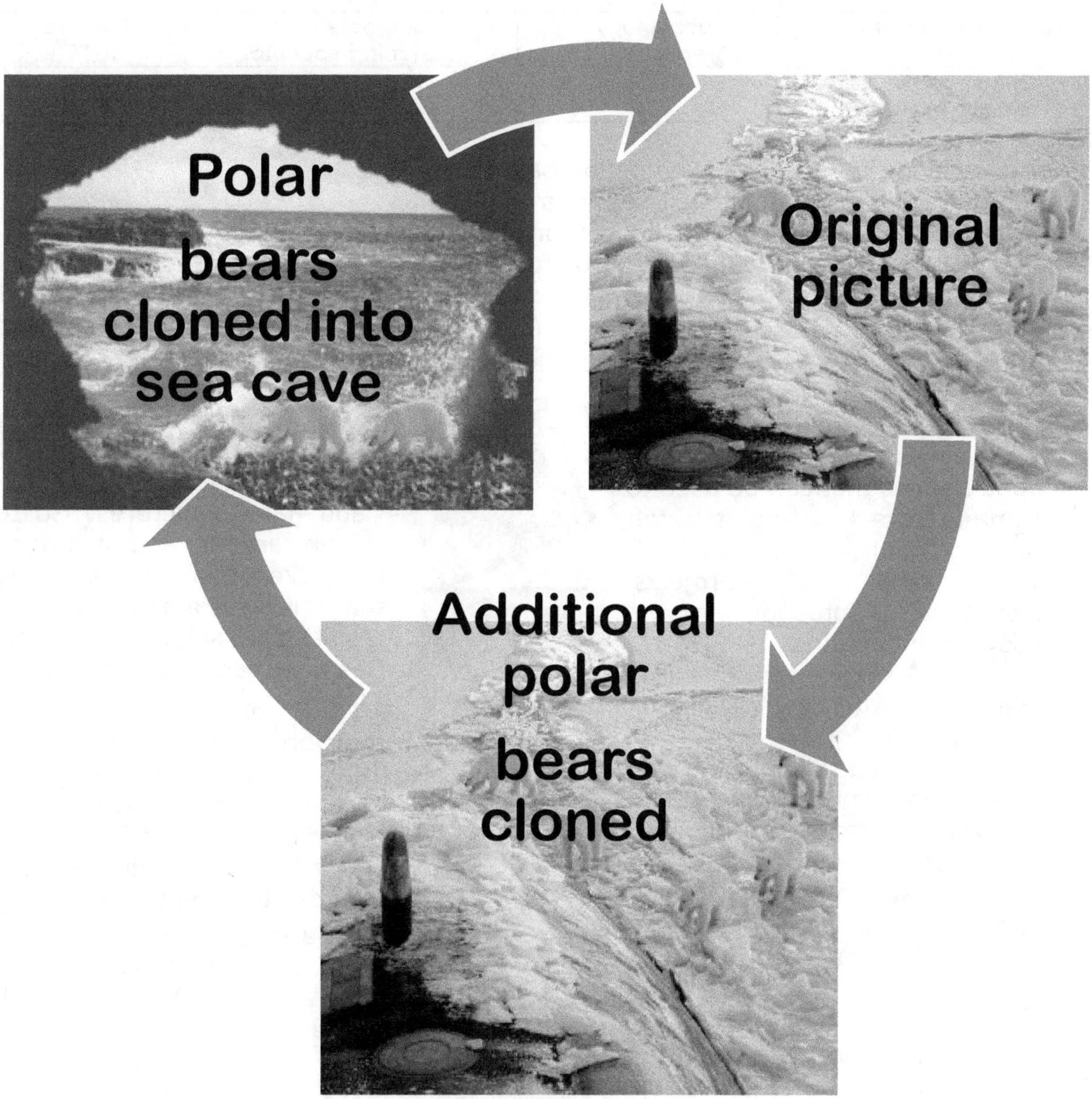

Subject #1: Art/Graphics

Project #9: Artistic Rendering in Photoshop. There are dozens of filters that add texture and overlays to pictures in Photoshop. Let students be as creative as they want. Discuss how each brings out a different emotion and/or meaning to the finished product. Take snapshots of each rendering

Higher-order thinking skills	Technology-specific:	Subject Area/ Learning-specific	Standard: ISTE
Applying information, creating knowledge	*photo editing,*	*Communication skills, creativity and innovation*	*6a-d*

Grade level: 5-8
Prior knowledge: Project 5 (Photoshop Basx)
Time required: 45 minutes, 2 sessions
Software required: Adobe Photoshop CS or higher (or your class photo editing tool)
Vocabulary: foreground, background, rendering, transparency, brush, font

Lesson Description

- Adobe Photoshop is the default photo-editing program for anyone serious about graphics. It not only fixes flaws, it creates unique appearances that can be used to communicate sophisticated and/or complicated ideas.
- This series of projects introduces Photoshop in an easy-to-understand way. Students learn the easiest skills, laid out for the best chance of success
- Introduce each skill in the order directed in this book (#5-#11). You will get less frustration and confusion from students.
- Demonstrate and then walk around classroom to be sure students find each tool

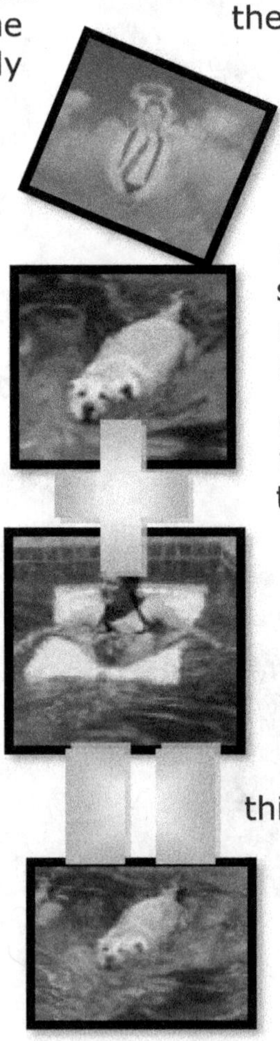

Computer Activity

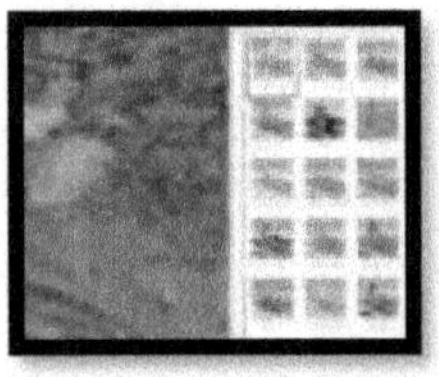

Note: If you don't use Photoshop, adapt this lesson to your preferred image editing tool.

- Adobe Photoshop (and many other image editors) has an impressive collection tools to add pizzazz to pics. Have students open their school picture for this project. They love working with their own image.
- #1: Artistic Renderings—add flair to pictures. Go to Filter—artistic and it brings up dozens of choices. Try some (it gives a preview of the result) and select a favorite. See next page for samples.
- #2: blur and smudge  tools on left tool bar to soften the background and sharpen a focal point. See next page for samples.
- #3: Use Filter-render-clouds to create a cloudy background (the colors of your foreground and background tool). Sample on this page.
- #4: Use the transparency tool  to adjust image visibility. Select one picture for the background (Pool Girl). Add another picture as a layer on top (Swimming Dog) and adjust its

transparency so that the under layer shows through.

- #5: Use the custom shape tool  to add shapes to the picture (see crown and fence below).

Extensions

- Add text with the text tool. You can adjust font, color, and warp.

Troubleshooting Tips

- *I can't get the right colors for the clouds (check your foreground and background tools. That's where Photoshop takes the colors)*
- *I'm trying to drag the picture but I get an error message (Check your layers. Do you have the correct layer highlighted?)*

Subject #1: Art/Graphics

Project #10: Drawing in Photoshop. Photoshop's reputation as a photo editor ignores its many other tools that enable you to draw like a pro with a wide variety of brushes, textures, and scintillating extras. This side of Photoshop is perfect for creative projects that tie in with different classroom lesson plans.

Higher-order thinking skills	Technology-specific:	Subject Area/ Learning-specific	Standard: ISTE
Applying information, creating knowledge	*photo editing, graphic design*	*Communication skills, creativity and innovation*	*4a-b*

Grade level: 5-8
Prior knowledge: Project 5 (Photoshop Basx), Project 9 (Artistic Rendering)
Time required: 45 minutes
Software required: Photoshop (or your class photo editing tool)
Vocabulary: layers, foreground, pattern, stack, history, canvas, gradient

Lesson Description

- This series of projects (#5-#11) introduces Photoshop in an easy-to-understand way. Students learn easy skills organized for the best chance of success
- Introduce each skill as directed in this book. You will get less frustration and confusion from students.
- Demonstrate and then walk around to be sure students understand.

Computer Activity

Note: If you don't use Photoshop in your school, adapt this lesson to a preferred image editing tool.

- Try these skills, to add a layer or return to the original canvas with the 'History' tab.
- #1: Click Gradient Tool on left toolbar. Check selections at top . Click and drag the mouse across the canvas to color the background. Use presets or adjust your foreground and background to the colors you prefer.
- #2: Add a new layer with layer tool.

Use paint bucket to fill. It either fills with the foreground color or pattern of your choice.

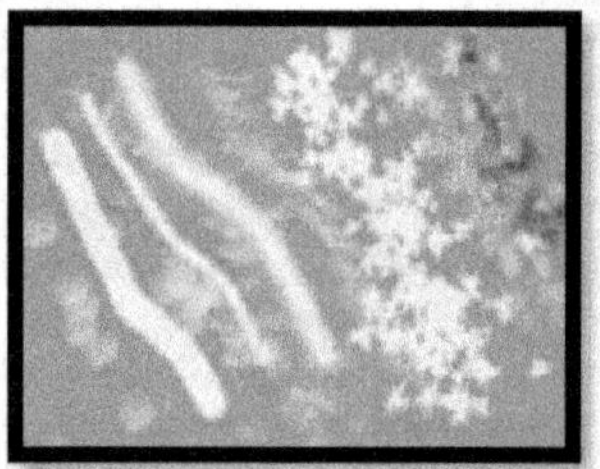

- #3: Add a new layer. Use paint brush and its options. Check the upper toolbar for selections.
- #4: Use drop down menu on top paint brush toolbar. Uncheck box for 'Show only current tool'. Try the circular rainbow and 'Starburst Color'.

Extensions

Drag the layer you like best (gradient, paint bucket, paint) to the top of the stack to make it visible. Or, click on the eye by layers you don't want and they'll become invisible.

Troubleshooting Tips

- *I can't paint on the canvas (Are you in the highlighted layer?)*

Samples of Drawing in Photoshop

Subject #1: Art/Graphics

Project #11: Photoshop Actions and the History Brush. These simple features (i.e., frames, quadrant colors, photo effects like snow) add professionalism to a finished product. This is a good addition to a Photoshop unit. It doesn't take much time to teach and its wow factor is off the charts with students.

Higher-order thinking skills	Technology-specific:	Subject Area/ Learning-specific	Standard: ISTE
Applying information, creating knowledge	*photo editing, graphic design*	*Communication skills, creativity and innovation*	*4a-d; 6a-d*

Grade level: 5-8
Prior knowledge: Project 5 (Photoshop Basx)
Time required: 45 minutes
Software required: Adobe Photoshop (or your class photo editing tool)
Vocabulary: History, sepia, quadrant, source, overlay, filter, layer, actions,

Lesson Description

- Photoshop is a robust drawing program with a massive variety of paint brushes, sprays, colors, gradients, to do whatever your brain dreams up. Pros love it.
- This lesson introduces challenging skills in an easy-to-understand way. It adds the 'wow' factor to learning with exercises as much about discovery as training.
- Demonstrate and then walk around to be sure students understand.

Computer Activity

Note: If you don't use Photoshop, adapt this lesson to your image editing tool.

- Photoshop Actions: These allow you to put a frame on a picture, recolor an image sepia or black and white, color by image quadrant, and more (see sample on this page). Go to the 'Actions' tab (next to 'History). Select 'Frames, Brushed Aluminum' or 'Quadrant Colors'. Push the 'Go' button at bottom.
- Photoshop History Brush: This enables you to set one picture as the source (like an anchor point in cloning), overlay an artistic effect and erase back to the source picture (see giraffes in middle—the vegetation appears blurry while the giraffes are crisp and clear). To do this, select 'Filter-Artistic-Fresco' to change the appearance of the giraffes. Select the History brush tool from the left toolbar and paint over the giraffes (by default it 'paints back' to the original picture). The original giraffes reappear while the background retains a Fresco look.

Extensions

- Change the History source position to one you've artistically rendered.

Troubleshooting Tips

- *I'm trying to paint the picture but nothing happens. (Is the correct layer highlighted?)*

Photoshop History Brush

Photoshop Actions

Subject #1: Art/Graphics

Project #12: Creating Simple Shapes with Excel Excel is a sure way to get students excited about math. Start with drawing simple pictures (because youngers love art). It's easier in Excel than on blank paper because Excel's grid lines are like graph paper. As students get older, use Excel to introduce the concept of graphs, grids, cells, rows, columns, coordinates, scale, etc.

Higher-order thinking skills	Technology-specific:	Subject Area/ Learning-specific	Standard: ISTE
See patterns, evaluate, understand	*Excel cells, paint bucket,*	*Math, prepares students for tessellations, critical thinking*	*5a, 6a, 6c*

Grade level: 2-7
Prior knowledge: Excel Basx
Time required: 45 minutes
Software required: Excel (or your class spreadsheet tool)
Vocabulary: cells, rows, columns, width, fill, paint bucket, autoshape, grid

Lesson Description

- This prepares youngers for graphs and data in upper grades.

Computer Activity

Note: Adapt this lesson to your spreadsheet program.

- Open Excel. Provide an overview of rows, columns, toolbars.
- Older students: Set the cells as squares to simulate graph paper by selecting the entire worksheet (click the cell where column A and row 1 meet). Now click the line between column A and B to find pixel width (probably 64). Click the line between row 1 and 2 and drag it down until it, too, is 64.

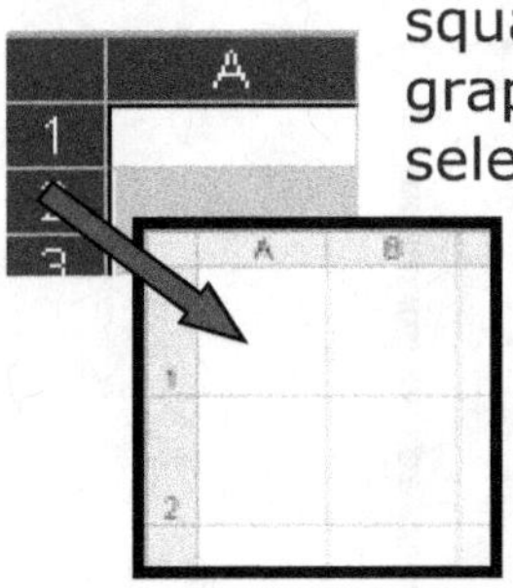

- Have students select a cell. Click the fill tool . Show them how to change the color with the drop-down arrow. Recolor.
- Color cells to create a square. Then change it to a rectangle.
- Now have students create their own drawings, using a variety of colors and cells. Use critical thinking skills to determine which cells and what colors to choose.

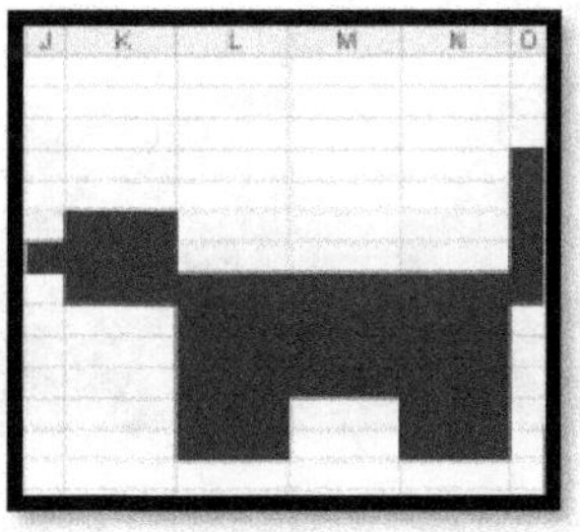

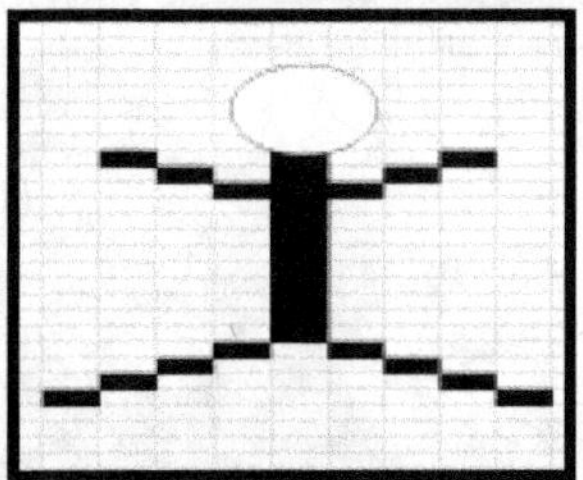

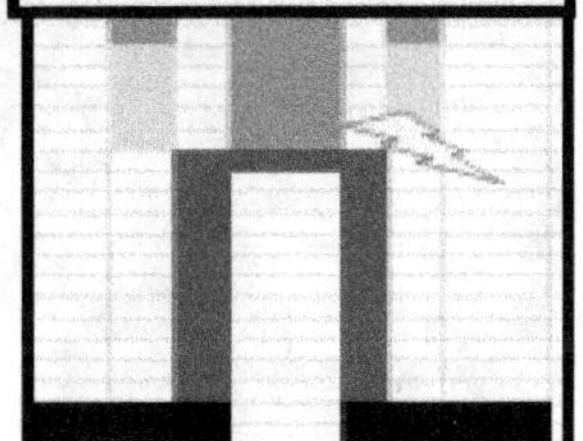

- Encourage students to resize the rows and columns as needed to make drawings more realistic.

Extensions

- Students can add autoshapes and freeform lines to drawings.

Troubleshooting Tips

- *I don't like the fill I used (Ctrl+Z to undo or select the cell and change to 'no fill'.)*
- *How do I select multiple cells? (Ctrl+click)*

Extra: Discover a hidden holiday picture

Students as young as 2nd grade follow the directions and uncover a surprise while they learn to use Excel rows, columns and paint bucket

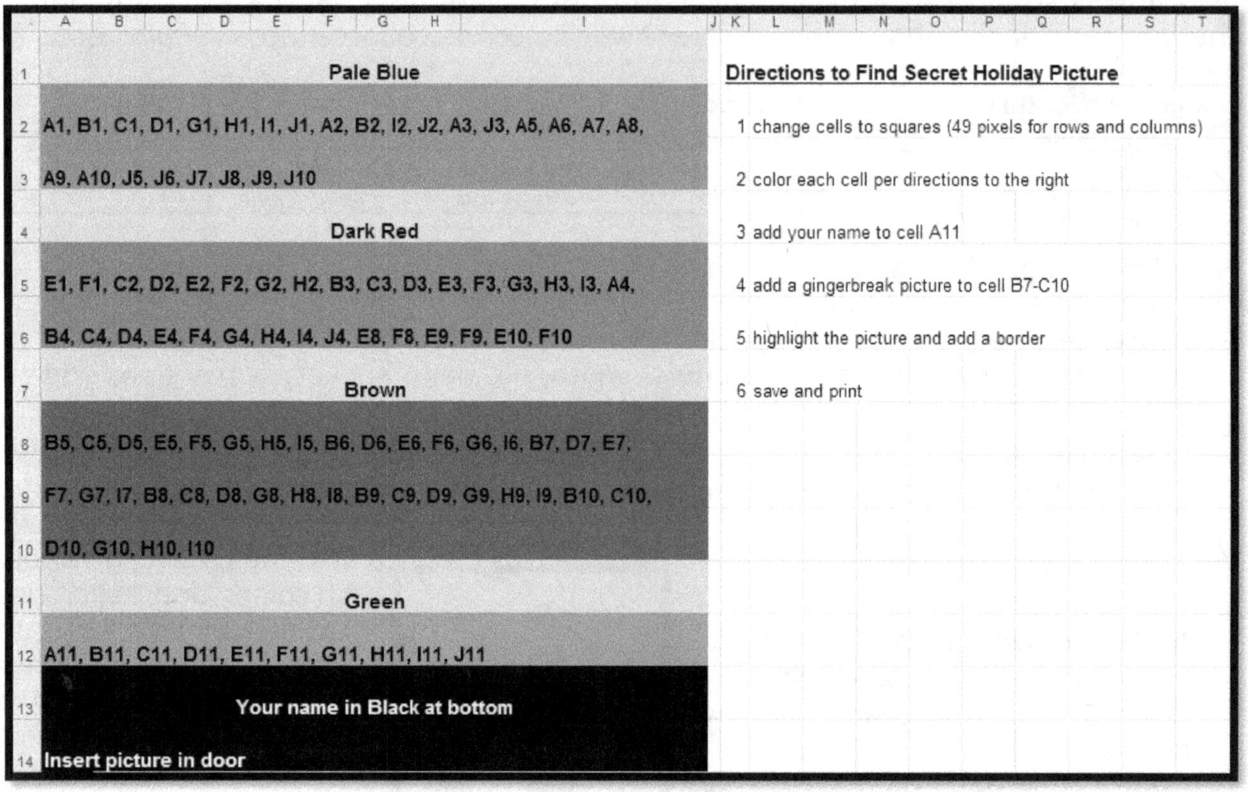
Pale Blue

A1, B1, C1, D1, G1, H1, I1, J1, A2, B2, I2, J2, A3, J3, A5, A6, A7, A8, A9, A10, J5, J6, J7, J8, J9, J10

Dark Red

E1, F1, C2, D2, E2, F2, G2, H2, B3, C3, D3, E3, F3, G3, H3, I3, A4, B4, C4, D4, E4, F4, G4, H4, I4, J4, E8, F8, E9, F9, E10, F10

Brown

B5, C5, D5, E5, F5, G5, H5, I5, B6, D6, E6, F6, G6, I6, B7, D7, E7, F7, G7, I7, B8, C8, D8, G8, H8, I8, B9, C9, D9, G9, H9, I9, B10, C10, D10, G10, H10, I10

Green

A11, B11, C11, D11, E11, F11, G11, H11, I11, J11

Your name in Black at bottom

Insert picture in door

Directions to Find Secret Holiday Picture

1 change cells to squares (49 pixels for rows and columns)

2 color each cell per directions to the right

3 add your name to cell A11

4 add a gingerbreak picture to cell B7-C10

5 highlight the picture and add a border

6 save and print

Subject #1: Art

Project #13: Art Online. Visit online resources from great world-wide museums. Take one lesson to introduce students to the six art sites I've listed (five to ten minutes on each) and then allow them to revisit when they have a few minutes at the end of a class project, unit, before lunch, or any other sponge time.

Higher-order thinking skills	Technology-specific:	Subject Area/ Learning-specific	Standard: ISTE
Comprehension—grasp meaning, interpret facts	*Broaden understanding of subjects, select/use applications productively*	*Find and enter addresses; use the toolbar, hyperlinks,*	*4a-d*

Grade level: K-8
Prior knowledge: Project 99 (Internet Basx) – if you have Book II of this collection
Time required: 45 minutes
Software required: Internet
Vocabulary: Internet, browser, online, back arrow, link, click, search

Lesson Description

- This list of sites is culled from the many available. They're geared for elementary learners, with minimum ads and maximum entertainment to draw children into the beauty and learning that is art.

Computer Activity

- To access the websites, Ctrl+click on the links below and they'll take you to the site. Or, Ctrl+click the images.
- Add the site to your favorites, your class website, or another link curator.
- Now take your time. Explore the links. Try the activities. Read what's offered.

Troubleshooting Tips

- *The address doesn't work. (Type it into the search engine. You'll get a list of suggested hits. Click on the one closest to the link here.)*
- *I don't like this webpage (use the back arrow to go back one page at a time)*

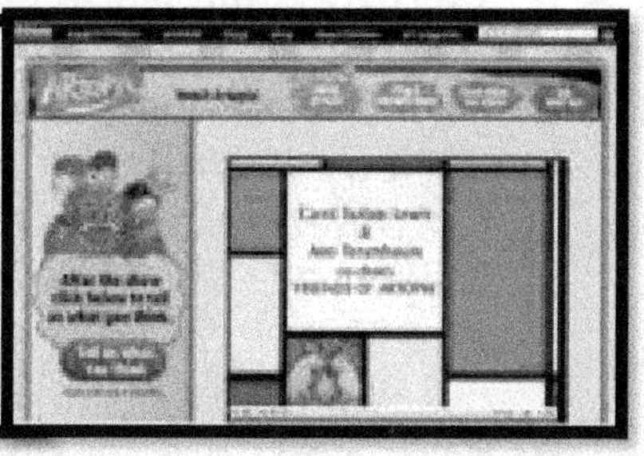

Google Art Project
Welcome to Artopia!
Starfall—Art Gallery for Kids

Subject #1: Art/Graphics

Project #14: Sponge Activities for Drawing and Graphics. Have students try these drawing and graphics programs when they have a few minutes at the end of the lesson, before lunch, during sponge time.

Higher-order thinking skills	Technology-specific:	Subject Area/ Learning-specific	Standard: ISTE
Apply (use methods in new situations)	*Use technology to broaden understanding*	*Coordinate with classroom teacher on topics*	*1d*

Grade level: K-8
Prior knowledge: Project 90 and 99 from Book II; 1 and 2 (KidPix Basx)
Time required: 20 minutes
Software required: Internet
Vocabulary: wallpaper, screen, download, icon, pin, GIF, Ctrl, zoom,

Lesson Description

- Art engages students in learning as a break from cerebral activities like math and science.
- There are many easy-to-use drawing programs online. When students complete a class activity, let them go into one of these drawing programs for a few minutes of inquiry-based learning:
    - *ABCYa Paint–great for Chromebooks*
    - *Drawing Melody–make music while you draw*
    - *Quick Draw–draw a picture while Google figures out what it is.*
    - *Sketchpad–some stamps, varied brushes; good for Chromebooks*
    - *Stickman–draw a stick figure and the site animates it*
- Be sure icons are on the desktop or pinned to the start menu to be easily found.
- Once I've shown students how to open and use these programs, I encourage their critical thinking and problem-solving skills by asking them to work without assistance—remember how they used it last time and do that again. Not surprisingly, recall is excellent if they want to use the program.

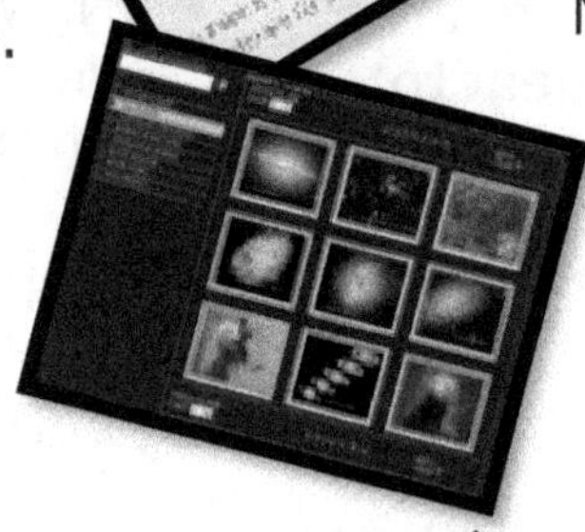

Extensions

- Have a list of wallpaper sites like NationalGeographic. Allow students to find pictures to use as wallpaper for their screen (for how to do this, visit Project 90 in Volume II). Give them a theme or pursue a topic they're covering in class.
- Need animated GIF's for PowerPoint slideshows or emails? There are lots of those sites available—another good way to soak up 5-10 minutes at the end of class

Troubleshooting Tips

- *I can't see the entire webpage (Zoom with Ctrl+-)*
- *Where'd the picture go I saved for wallpaper (check My Pictures)*

Subject #2: Composition and Communication

Project #15: A Holiday Letter in Word. Students write a letter paying attention to correct greeting, body, closing, then format with fonts, colors, border, pictures, a watermark (grades 4-6), and wraps (grades 4-6). For grade 2-3, write the letter one lesson; format the next. Olders: Do both in one lesson.

Higher-order thinking skills	Technology-specific:	Subject Area/ Learning-specific	Standards: ISTE
Using knowledge student has learned; organizing information	*Word: change fonts/ colors/sizes Tech: save to flash drive*	*Letter-writing Grammar/spelling*	*1c, 1d, 4a*

Grade level: 2-6
Prior knowledge: Introduction to MS Word
Time required: 45 minutes for grades 3-6, 2-45 minute sessions for grade 2
Software required: MS Word (or your class word processing tool)
Vocabulary: greeting, body, closing, indent, tab, icon, font, network, flash drive, dialogue box, flash drive, border

Lesson Description

- This is an exploration of authentic questions to engage students in active learning.
- Writing includes a thank-you, memory, wish, or a holiday-appropriate topic.

Computer Activity

- Discuss letter-writing.
- In your class word processing program, start with a heading (name, teacher, date).
- Add a greeting ('Dear **') on a separate line, font size 14-18, any font.
- Indent each paragraph of body with the tab key. Continue with font size 14-18, any font. Depending on grade level, remind students to capitalize the first letter of a sentence and proper nouns, add a space after periods and commas. Add closing.
- While typing, use good keyboarding skills. When completed, clear red squiggly lines (spelling errors) by right-clicking on the word and selecting the correct spelling.
- Add holiday border through 'Borders and Shading' dialogue box.
- Check work against the rubric in this book to be sure to follow all directions.

Extensions

- Change font color, font and size of five words to add emphasis. Show how by clicking inside the word or highlighting it. Be creative but appropriate to the holiday (i.e. 'chiller' fits Halloween, not Easter.)
- Add clipart to body (not heading, greeting or closing). Explain how clipart goes where cursor is blinking.
- For more experienced students, add a text box, footer, WordArt title, watermark and/or autoshape.

Troubleshooting Tips

- *What's the keyboard shortcut for date (Shift+Alt+D)*

Second grade

Zoom in if needed

Assessment 1—Story rubric

***Name*________________________ *Teacher's Name*____________________**

HOLIDAY STORY
GRADING RUBRIC

1. Heading with name, date, teacher __________
2. Title stands out, centered __________
3. Several lines of story __________
    a. 3 different fonts __________
    b. 3 different size fonts __________
    c. 3 different colors __________
    d. Spell-check __________
    e. Grammar-check __________
4. 1-3 inline pictures __________
5. A festive border __________
6. Story fills one page but not more __________
7. Professional appearance __________

Third-Sixth grade

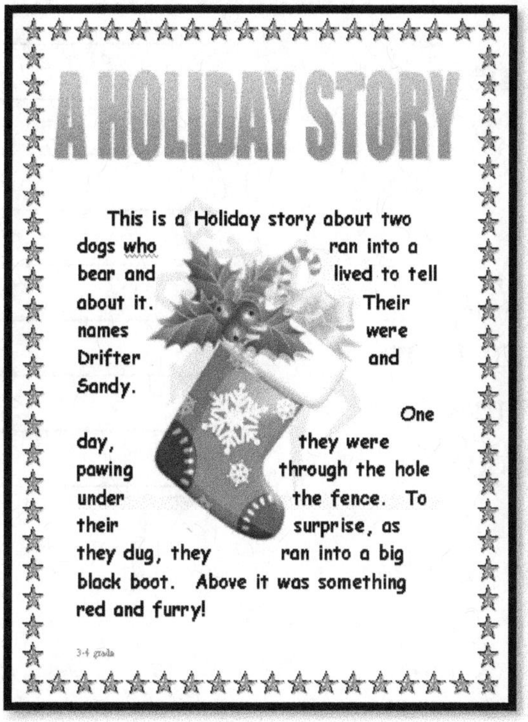

Name ______________________

Teacher's Name ______________

HOLIDAY STORY

3rd-6th GRADING RUBRIC

1.	Heading with name, date, teacher	________
2.	Several lines of story	________
	a. 5 different fonts	________
	b. 5 different size fonts	________
	c. 5 different colors	________
	d. Spell-check	________
	e. Grammar check	________
3.	A festive border	________
4.	A WordArt title	________
5.	5 pictures—all the same size	________
6.	*Text box with a quote or bullets**	________
7.	Watermark	________
8.	Footer	________
9.	*Autoshape with fill color**	________
10.	Story fills page, but not more	________
	a. Check Print Preview	________
11.	Professional appearance	________

*Italics indicate Extra Credit

6 MS Word Tricks Every Student Should Know

The faster you teach students to be problem solvers, the more they'll learn. Computers are a foreign language. Even with small class sizes, the more students can do for themselves, the more fun they'll have learning the intricacies of technology.

The good news is, students love to be independent. They find it cool to know keyboard shortcuts for getting stuff done. In my class, students can help their neighbors, and they love showing off their problem solving skills. Here are 9 tricks that cover many common problems students will face using MS Word:

1. **Ctrl+Z–undo**
   This will be their favorite. There are too many times to mention when I've had a frantic student, almost in tears because s/he thought s/he'd lost his/her document, and two seconds later, I retrieved it. I was the hero for a class period.

2. **How to find lost documents**
   It takes a while for users to get accustomed to saving files on a network. Often, documents end up lost (in my school, students must drill down through five levels to get to their unique location). My students learn early to use '**search**' on the start menu.

3. **How to insert data**
   The 'insert' key is so confusing I'm told it is being de-activated in the future. If students complain they lose data as they type, this is probably why. Show them how to **push the 'insert' key** and all will be fixed.

4. **Show-hide tool.**
   Kids try to strong-arm Word into doing their will–often the wrong way. My favorite is 'enter enter' as a shortcut to double space. It seems to work until they must edit the document, and then everything gets messed up. Have students push the **show-hide button** to see if they're using the double space tool. Then, show them where the icon is.

5. **Tables—they work so much better than columns and tabs.**
   Teach it to kids **early and use it often**. It will save miles of distress.

6. **How to insert the date**
   It takes until Middle School for students to remember the date. Before that, they will always ask. Show them the **Shift+Alt+D** shortkey that inserts the current date into Word. They love it and it saves a lot of time for you.

Subject #2: Composition and Communication

Project #16: A Holiday Memory in Word or KidPix. Write a holiday memory letter, with your picture, text wrapped around it, and additional formatting. This reinforces writing skills as well as technology.

Higher-order thinking skills	Technology-specific:	Subject Area/ Learning-specific	Standard: ISTE
Applying information, creating	*Editing text, formatting documents, basic graphic skills*	*Letter writing Grammar/spelling*	*1d, 4a*

Grade level: 1-5
Prior knowledge: Intro to Word, #1/2: KidPix Basx #15: Holiday Letter in Word
Time required: 45 minutes
Software required: MS Word, KidPix (or your class word processing and art tools)
Vocabulary: wrap, heading, greeting, closing, font,

Lesson Description

- This project is a greeting to the student's family--a thank-you, a memory, a wish, or another holiday-appropriate topic.
- Student decides between Word or KidPix: Select KidPix to communicate with pictures, MS Word to communicate with words.
- Student works independently as much as possible. This is similar to #15 so student can recall those skills. Students decide which program suits his/her needs. Is it art or words? When s/he's decided, open Word or KidPix

Computer Activity

Note: This works fine with other word processing and art programs.

- Word: Add name/teacher/date as a heading (font size 12, TNR); include all parts of a letter (greeting, 60-8 sentence body, closing). For body: Use font size 36-48, any font and color. From Project 15, remember how to insert a border, change fonts/color/sizes, add pictures. Expect students to remember or ask neighbors for help.
- KidPix: Use ABC text tool for a brief greeting. Decorate with a personal photo, sticker—frames, and the paint bucket fill (third bucket).
- Print without help; save to student folder; save-as to flash drive; print

Extensions

- MS Word: Add a watermark, footer, autoshape (fill the autoshape with color), text box,
- KidPix: Change the font look, color and size. Add student name with animation tool (the dog)—alphabet

Troubleshooting Tips

- *To change font, size, color in Word, click inside a word and select font/size/color. This is a quick way to format without highlighting a word.*
- *I can't move the photo I added to KidPix. (When you Add-add graphic and insert the photo, make sure it's placed and resized to your taste before clicking out of it. Otherwise, use the Oops Guy and start over.)*
- *Trouble getting started:*

  - *I can't exit (Alt+F4)*
  - *I can't print (Ctrl+P, file-print)*

Dear Mother and Father
I remember last Christmas, when THE NEW PUPPY ate my
didn't even cry. hope you
great
Dhristmas.
love max
ps I appreciate
you have d
for me.

Dear Mom and Dad,
Happy holidays! I member
last year when we didn't have
Sid. I got to eat all my cookies
by myself!
I wish you a merry Christmas, and I
hope this is your best Christmas
ever! And thank you for all
the presents you gave me.
Love, Me

Happy Holiday
Love
Me

Subject #2: Composition and Communication

Project #17: A Holiday Story in Word. A review of MS Word writing skills emphasizing knowledge student has collected and established learning outcomes

Higher-order thinking skills	Technology-specific:	Subject Area/ Learning-specific	Standard: ISTE
Using knowledge student has learned	*MS word: change fonts/ colors/sizes*	*Letter-writing Grammar/spelling*	*1d, 4a, 4b*

Grade level: 2-7
Prior knowledge: Introduction to MS Word, Project 16: A Holiday Memory in Word
Time required: 25-45 minutes
Software required: MS Word (or your class word processing tool)
Vocabulary: font, font size, cursor, double space, heading, greeting, setting, plot, text box, call-out,

Lesson Description

- A holiday story or letter with pictures, border, varied fonts/colors/ sizes, and a WordArt title (for story).
- Second graders hone basics. Older grades add to Word skillset.
- Students work without teacher assistance as much as possible, relying on already-accumulated knowledge.

Computer Activity

Note: This works fine with other word processing programs, i.e., Google Docs.

- Open Word. Add heading (name, teacher, date on three lines), font size 12, Times New Roman.
- Double space between sections, i.e., heading and greeting. Student can select font size 14-36, any font, for balance of letter/story.
- Review parts of a letter—greeting, body, closing
- Review parts of a story: character, setting, plot, crisis, resolution.

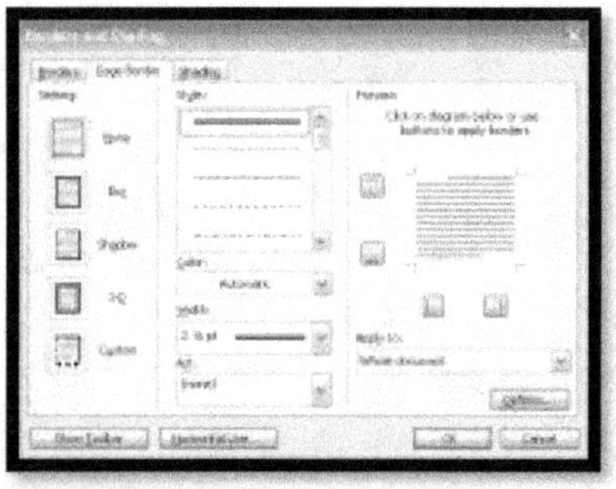

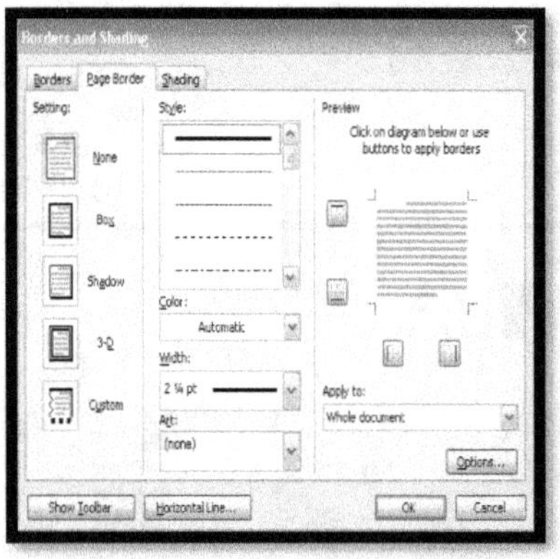

- Have at least one paragraph, 3-8 sentences, depending upon grade.
- Challenge students to add:
  - art borders (see inset)
  - pictures (place cursor where image goes)
  - 5 fonts/color/sizes
- Review before printing. Clear red squiggly lines by correcting spelling
- Story must fill one page, but no more. Resize pictures as needed. Print preview before printing.

Extensions

- Add text box, call-out.
- Color the text box and call-out.

Troubleshooting Tips

- *To change font, size, color, click inside word and select font/size/color. This is a quick way without having to highlight the word.*
- *Trouble finishing up:*
  - *I can't exit (Alt+F4)*
  - *I can't print (Ctrl+P, file-print)*

Second Grade:

Name
Teacher
Date

HALLOWEEN

Once there was a ghost, a and a pumpkin. They lived in a haunted house.

Guess what their favorite holiday was?

Third Grade:

Your name__________
Your teacher__________
Date__________

Halloween Story

One spooky Halloween a little boy and his friends went out for a fun night of trick o treating. Little did they know it would be a night THEY would not soon forget!!! It was a very scary night.

Fourth-Seventh Grade:

Your name
Your teacher
Today's date

Dear Mom and Dad,

THANKSGIVING is fun, isn't it! I love you. We are going to have a really good time. I think about all the food we are going to have, the turkey and mashed potatoes, and then serve dinner at the shelter by Grampa's. That's the best part—sharing.

Happy Thanksgiving!

Love Me

Fifth-Seventh Grade:

Your name
Your teacher
Date

HALLOWEEN STORY

A man was walking home alone late one night when he hears ..... BUMP... BUMP... BUMP...

...behind him. He looks back, and sees a coffin banging towards him.

BUMP... BUMP... BUMP...

Terrified, the man runs home, coffin bouncing behind him ... . faster... BUMP... BUMP... BUMP.

He fumbles with his keys, rushes in, and locks the door. The coffin crashes through his door, lid clapping ...

clappity-BUMP... CLAPPITY-BUMP... clappity-BUMP

His heart's pounding; head reeling; breath coming in sobbing gasps. With a loud CRASH the coffin comes bumping and clapping towards him. Desperate, he throws a basket of Halloween candy at the apparition.

Now what happens???

Happy Halloween

Subject #2: Composition and Communication

Project #18: Holiday Greetings in Word, KidPix . Another holiday letter, but this time, student decides to share his/her thoughts with text or pictures.

Higher-order thinking skills	Technology-specific:	Subject Area/ Learning-specific	Standard: ISTE
Communication of ideas, info *Problem-solving*	*Add/edit text* *Format doc (fonts, borders)* *Save to flash drive* *Mouse skills; tool bars skills*	*Composition* *Creative writing* *Grammar/spelling* *Art*	*4a, 4b, 6a*

Grade level: 2-4
Prior knowledge: Intro to Word, Intro to KidPix, several projects in each
Time required: 45 minutes
Software required: KidPix, MS Word (or your class word processing and art tools)
Vocabulary: tools, border, font, export, greeting, body, closing, highlight

Lesson Description

- This summative asks student to choose Word or KidPix as a medium to express their thoughts.
- Words or pictures—which better facilitates active learning? Both encourage multimedia communication skills with text, color, graphics.
- Word offers an in-depth exploration of dynamic topics with the addition of borders and watermarks (for those capable of these skills). KidPix removes the pressure of not-quite-developed writing strategies and allows students to engage in nonverbal communication (which, by the way, accounts for more than half of all communication).
- Student decides which program suits his/her need, and then opens.

Computer Activity

Note: This works fine with other word processing programs, i.e., Google Docs.

- KidPix: Students use only those tools s/he remembers. Try some, explore, don't be afraid to make mistakes. Take the entire 45 minute class. Any amount of text and pictures is fine.
- MS Word: Students include all parts of a letter (greeting, body—6-8 sentences, close), font size 48, any font look and color.
- Do you remember how to insert a border? Change fonts/color/sizes? Add pictures?
- Student works independently, without teacher assistance as much as possible. Act as their guide, mentor, not keeper-of-all-knowledge.
- Correct spelling before printing. Print without help. Save to student network folder; save-as to flash drive.

Extensions

- Have experienced students add more detail to their letter—memories, stories, whatever tells parents better why s/he loves them (see example on next page)

Troubleshooting Tips

- *To change font, size, color, just click inside the word and select font/size/color. This is a quick way to change a word without highlighting it.*

Holiday greeting: K-1 at top, 2-4 at bottom

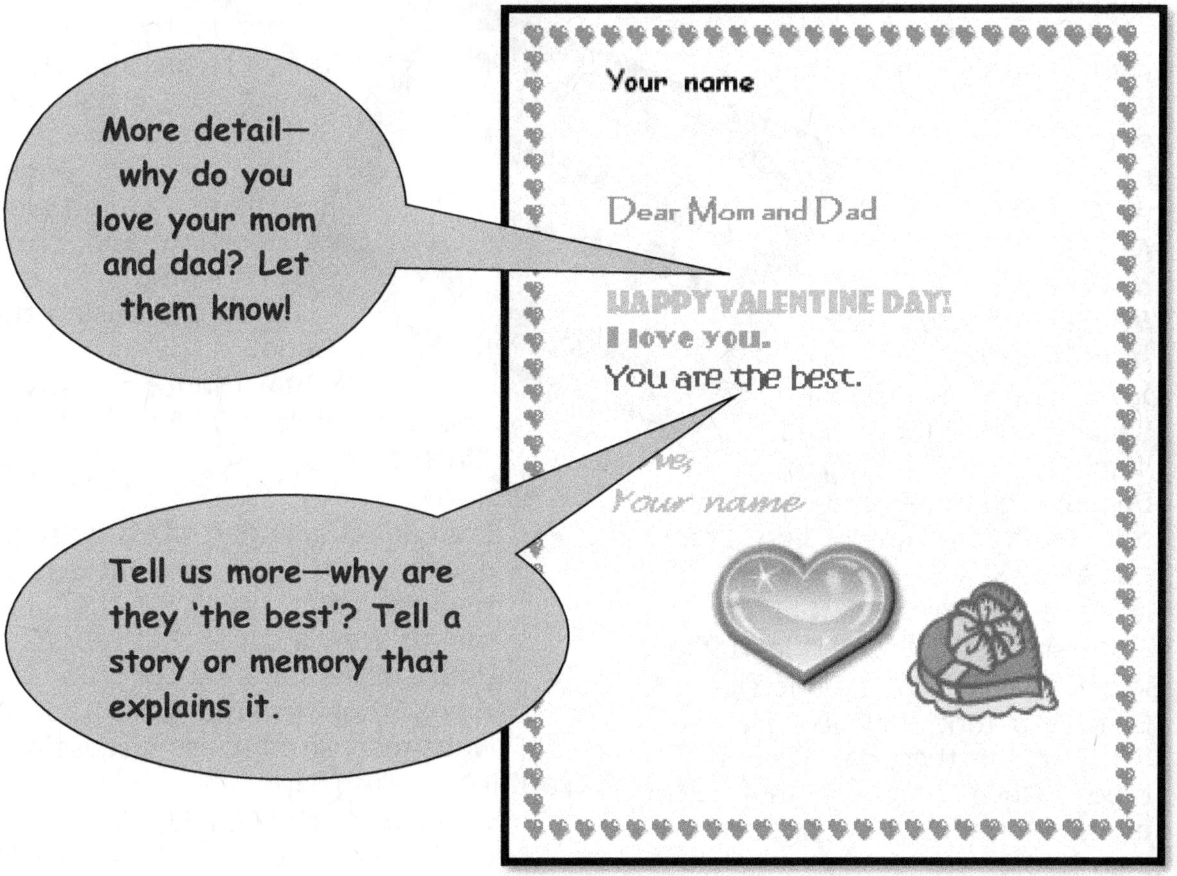

Subject #2: Composition and Communication

Project #19: My Book cover (in KidPix) Draw a cover for a class project or unit of inquiry, or use a template. Have students mix text and pictures for an attractive design. Use this project to introduce KidPix fonts, font sizes, font colors to grade 1.

Higher-order thinking skills	Technology-specific:	Subject Area/ Learning-specific	Standard: ISTE
See patterns, understand information	*Text, formatting, KidPix basics, multimedia communication*	*Spelling, creative writing, communication*	*1d, 4b*

Grade level: 1-2
Prior knowledge: Project 1, 2: KidPix Basx I and II
Time required: 15 minutes, 2 sessions
Software required: KidPix (or your class art tool)
Vocabulary: book cover, category, template, background tool, font, text tool

Lesson Description

- Create a fairy tale/fable story cover to support discussion in language arts. With one picture, students communicate their understanding of a topic they've spent several weeks discussing, reading about, exploring.
- Students share ideas not with words but the stimulating environment of art.

Computer Activity

Note: Other drawing tools can be used if you don't have KidPix.

- Open KidPix. Select the background tool and 'Fantasy' category. Encourage students to try as many templates as they'd like before deciding.
- Select a background that fits the understanding of fairy tales/fables.
- Select the Text tool, font size 72. Choose a font they like from the list. Click on their background and type, 'Once upon a time…' (or another name as directed by instructor).
- Critically evaluate the work. Is it large enough? Does it show up against the background? To make changes, highlight the text and select a different font/color/size. Be sure student name is on cover (font size 12).
- Student works independently, without teacher assistance, as much as possible. If they have problems, ask them to engage their problem-solving and critical thinking skills before raising their hand.
- Print without help; save to student network folder; save-as to flash drive

Extensions

- Instead of using a preconstructed background, have student use the realistic paint brush or the pencil tool to draw a cover that represents their understanding of the title. Have them think back to the websites visited, class discussions.

Troubleshooting Tips

- *I can't exit (Alt+F4)*
- *I can't print (Ctrl+P, file-print)*

Two KidPix Book covers

Top: using background

Bottom: using paint brush

Subject #2: Composition and Communication

Project #20: A Holiday Card—in KidPix. Mix words and pictures to create a holiday card using skills learned since the school year began. Students can also add paint bucket backgrounds and fills to extend the lesson.

Higher-order thinking skills	Technology-specific:	Subject Area/ Learning-specific	Standard: ISTE
Creating knowledge (recall info)	*Format pictures, merge multiple intelligences*	*Grammar and spelling*	*1d, 4b*

Grade level: K-3
Prior knowledge: Project 1/2 (KidPix Basx I/II)
Time required: 30 minutes, 2 sessions for K-1
Software required: KidPix (or your class art tool)
Vocabulary: grammar, capitalize, shift key, caps lock, fill, palette, toolbar, tool

Lesson Description

- Cards are created using a variety of mediums (paint brush, fills, text, backgrounds). For younger students, use two sessions: one for practice and one to redo and print. This gives ample time for all KidPix's tools.
- Encourage creativity. They draw a picture, a symbol, the shape of words, whatever comes to mind.
- As the year progresses, ask them to work independently, as much as possible. By the third or fourth card, they should have a toolkit of problem-solving skills to turn to before engaging teacher-controlled learning.

Computer Activity

Note: Other drawing tools can be used if you don't have KidPix.

- Open KidPix. Decide between paint brush and pencil tool. If they pick pencil, encourage them to use all tools on the bottom toolbar. If they pick paint, suggest they use at least 5 paint brushes.
- Students enhance drawings with the spray can (if you've covered it in class), fill tool, stamps and stickers.
- If student can't remember how to perform a skill, ask questions to help recall. Remind them when they used it last. Act as a guide, not a giver-of-knowledge. If they still can't remember, suggest they try what they do remember. There is no right or wrong choice.
- Add text. Display a list of words used in class on the overhead. Remind them how important spelling is. For younger students, use caps lock. For older students, use the shift key to capitalize the first letter of a sentence and proper nouns, and put a period at the end of the sentence.

- Print without help; save

Extensions

- Change font and font color for the sentence or their name.

Troubleshooting Tips

- *My shift key doesn't work (Is caps lock on?)*
- *I can't change the color of my words (Highlight)*

Subject #2: Composition and Communication

Project #21: A Holiday Card in Publisher. Create a holiday card using Publisher templates. Make it simple for youngers (don't edit text, add only one picture). Let olders change as much as they wish. Use this lesson to teach youngers about templates and olders about design and menus. This project is very easy, an authentic representation of how fun computers are.

Higher-order thinking skills	Technology-specific:	Subject Area/ Learning-specific	Standard: ISTE
Analyzing, organizing parts	*Using and editing templates, the three c's,*	*Grammar and spelling, critical thinking*	*1d, 4b, 6a*

Grade level: 2-6
Prior knowledge: Introduction to Publisher, Project 22 (A Holiday Flier)
Time required: 20-30 minutes, depending upon the skill of the student
Software required: Publisher (or your class Desktop Publishing tool)
Vocabulary: layout, template, place-savers, font scheme, color scheme, DTP, task pane, thumbnail, verse, trifold

Lesson Description

- Publisher is one of many desktop publishing (DTP) software programs that facilitate creation of brochures, magazines, newsletters, cards, fliers and more with easy-to-use, easy-to-personalize templates.
- While its strength for the educator's classroom is magazines, trifold brochures and newsletters, greeting cards are an engaging way for students to learn the program while they explore a real-world application. Greeting cards are simple to make, exciting for project-oriented students, and a fulfilling start to a robust, sometimes challenging program. The only easier skill is fliers, covered in Project 22.

- The template greeting card used in this project has a stock layout—colors and design elements arranged in an attractive layout—and a Hallmark-type greeting that can be rewritten to express the user's unique thoughts.

Computer Activity

Note: Other desktop publishing tools (like Canva) can be used if you don't have Publisher.

- Open Publisher. Select 'greeting cards—all holidays'
- Scroll through the available cards and select one with the desired layout.
- When it's selected, color and font options appear on the right side (called 'schemes'). Have student try different choices until they find one that fits their interpretation of the current holiday. Once they've selected it, push 'create' at bottom of screen.
- Take a quick tour of the greeting card screen
  - Cover comes up first. See the four views along the left sidebar—those are the card's pages.

- Notice the similarity between the menu bar at the top (the one with the words) and the ribbon (with the icon pictures) to those already used in MS Word.
- **Page 1** (cover): 2nd grade: Leave the picture and greeting unchanged. 3-6: Adjust as needed by replacing text and pictures. Go to page two.
- **Page 2** (blank, left inside): Add a holiday picture(s) from clipart (or Google images). Resize to fit page.
- **Page 3** (with a verse, right, inside): 2nd grade: make no changes. 3-6: Click to edit the message.
- **Page 4 (back):** Add creator's name
- Check grammar and spelling before printing. Save to student folder; save-as to flash drive
- Print. Have students fold it themselves (top down, side to side).

Extensions

- Change the greeting layout from the template page (before pushing 'create')
- Add a thumbnail picture on page four, above the creator's name (see sample below)

Troubleshooting Tips

- *Print preview has some pages upside down. (When you fold the card, these will work out).*

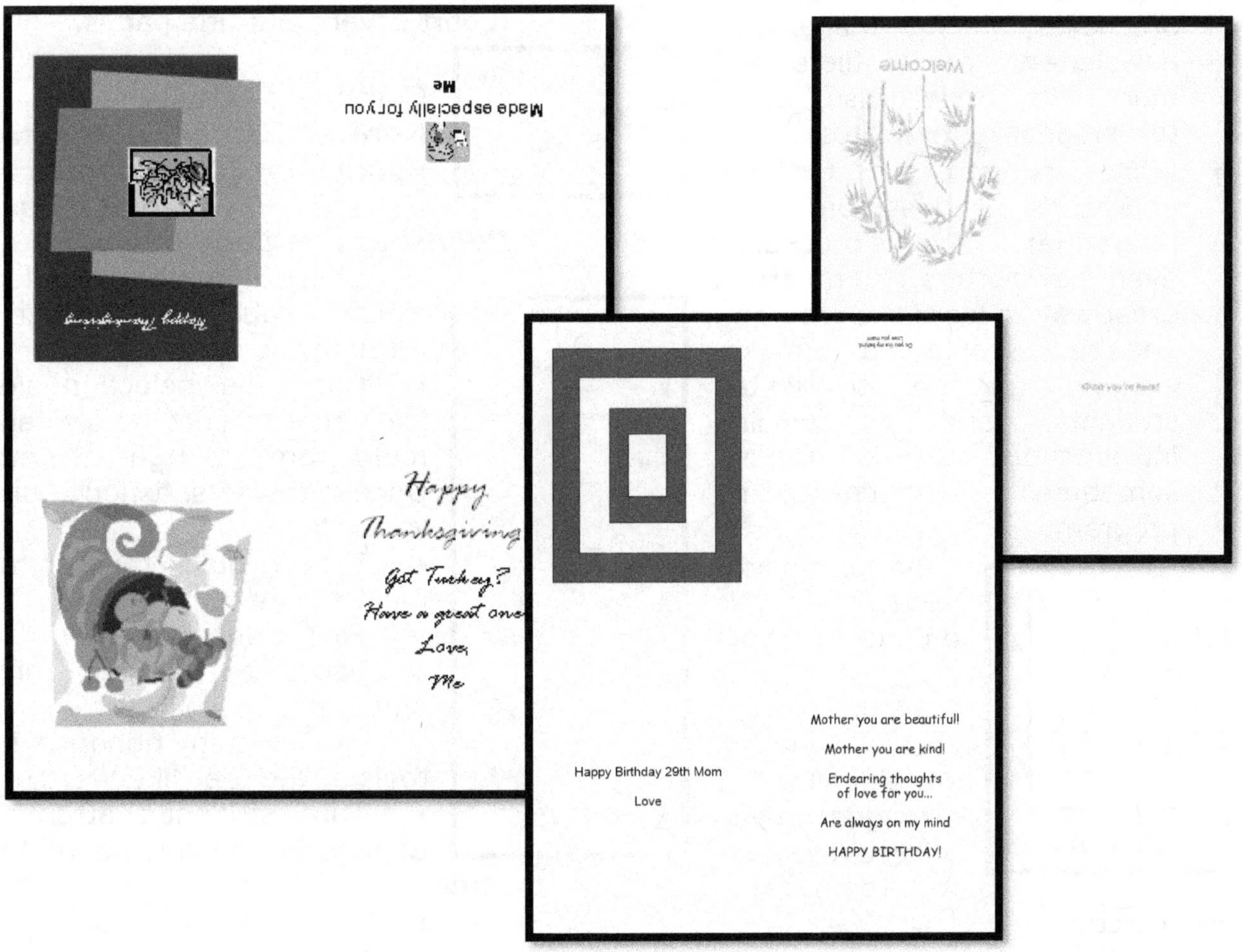

Subject #2: Composition and Communication

Project #22: A Holiday flier in Publisher. Create a holiday flier using Publisher. Choose a one-page template and adapt text and picture. Olders can adjust colors, fonts, etc. Use this lesson to teach youngers about templates and olders about design and menus. This project is very easy, an authentic representation of how fun computers are.

Higher-order thinking skills	Technology-specific:	Subject Area/ Learning-specific	Standard: ISTE
Analyzing, organizing parts	*Using templates, the three c's, editing templates,*	*Grammar and spelling, design layout*	*6a, 6c-d*

Grade level: 2-6
Prior knowledge: Introduction to Publisher
Time required: 15-30 minutes (depending upon skill level)
Software required: Publisher (or your class DTP tool)
Vocabulary: template, place-saver, thumbnail, full-size image, toolbar

Lesson Description

- What is Publisher? It's one of the many desktop publishing (DTP) software programs for creating brochures, magazines, newsletters, cards, fliers and more with easy-to-use, easy-to-personalize templates.
- While its strength for the educator's classroom is magazines, trifold brochures and even newsletters, fliers are a great way to learn the program. They're simple to make, exciting for project-oriented students, and a fulfilling introduction to a robust, sometimes challenging program.

Jungle Quick Publication

- The templates used in this project come with a stock layout—colors and design elements arranged in an attractive layout, with room for:
  - A picture
  - A text for a greeting
  - A sub-text for student name and information
- These templates are also useful for report covers and title pages.

Computer Activity

Note: Other desktop publishing (DTP) tools can be used if you don't have Publisher like Canva.

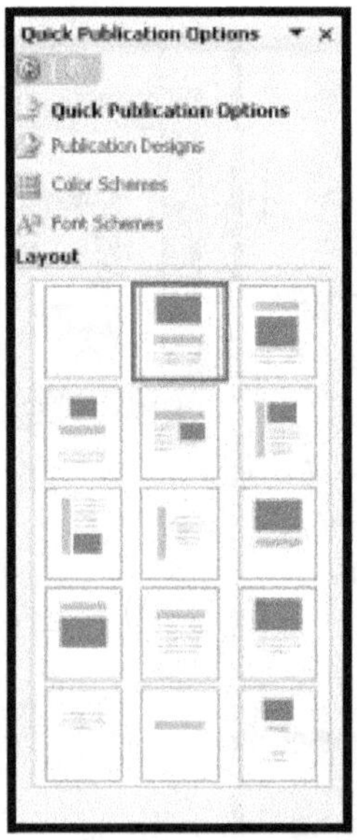

- Open Publisher. Select 'Quick Publications'. Scroll through the options.
- Click the selection you like, then select colors and fonts from the right column. Once you're satisfied, click 'create'
- Take a quick tour of the main screen:
  - Flier in the center.
  - Pages on the left (only one in this case).
  - Menus and ribbon with tools at the top (like Word)
- Turn student's attention to flier in the middle of the screen.

- 'Heading': Click this word and add a holiday greeting. Don't worry about size. It'll adjust as needed to fit the field.
- 'Sub-heading': Click and add a one or two-sentence greeting (including their name). Again, it adjusts to fit your message.
- Picture: Delete the stock picture and add a holiday image from clipart or Google images.
- Check grammar and spelling before printing. Save to student network folder and flash drive

Extensions

There aren't any.

Troubleshooting Tips

- *The font's too big. I ran out of room (Keep typing. It'll get smaller.)*
- *I found a picture on the internet and it doesn't work right on the template. (Be sure to use the full-size image—those free to the public—not the thumbnail. Click the thumbnail image once and again for the full-size image. If that doesn't work, resize the picture using the handles.)*

Clockwise: 2nd grade, 3rd grade, 4th grade, 5th grade:

Subject #2: Composition and Communication

Project #23: A Holiday Calendar in Publisher. Create a calendar of students holiday or summer activities. Students pick their template, add text and pictures. Pictures can be copy-pasted from an internet search. This is a popular project.

Higher-order thinking skills	Technology-specific:	Subject Area/ Learning-specific	Standard: ISTE
Analyzing, organizing parts	*Using templates, the three c's, editing templates, layout*	*Grammar and spelling*	*4a-b, 6.b*

Grade level: 4-7
Prior knowledge: Introduction to Publisher, Project 21/22: Holiday Card/Flier
Time required: 45 minutes
Software required: Publisher (or your class DTP tool)
Vocabulary: cell, font, template, image, row, range, scheme,

Lesson Description

- Publisher is a desktop publishing (DTP) software program used to create brochures, magazines, cards, newsletters, fliers and more with easy-to-use, easy-to-personalize templates.
- While its strength for educators is magazines and trifold brochures, calendars are a crowd pleaser, thus a great formative exercise and dynamic approach to experiential learning. They're simple but exciting while fostering creativity and providing a fulfilling introduction to a robust, sometimes challenging program.
- The templates used in this project come with a stock layout—colors and design elements arranged in an attractive layout, with room for:
    - One or more pictures
    - Daily and monthly events
- In this project, students make an events calendar to track each other's lives over the holidays.

- The 45 minutes suggested as time required is to allow students to engage in authentic, real-time discussions before filling in the blanks on the template. They will want plenty of time to share and discuss upcoming events.
- Make student contribution to the calendar's events list optional. Some students won't want to share and that's fine.

Computer Activity

Note: Other DTP tools, like Canva, can be used if you don't have Publisher.

- Open Publisher. Select 'Calendars'. Pick an appealing layout from center (pictures at the top or side, calendar size, etc.), then select colors and fonts from the right column (as done with the flier and greeting cards).

- Select 'One month per page'. Push button to 'Set Calendar Dates'. Pick current month.
- When that's done, click 'create'.
- Replace stock graphics with holiday pictures from clipart or Google images.
- Now it's time to fill in appointments. Point out the date cell. This is where events will go. Info must fit in this cell, so it must be brief. Students can adjust font size (10-12 is probably best) to suit how much they must write.
- Start with activities occurring at school—concerts, awards assemblies, dances, etc. Show students how to click after the correct date, push enter to start a new line, and add information.
- Take suggestions from students. Where are they going for the holidays? What birthdays are occurring? Whose grandparents are visiting? Only take one per date. Encourage students to enter their own appointments in place of class ones if they prefer.
- Have students add their name to an empty cell in the last row (see sample in lower right cell).
- *Save* to student network folder and back up to flash drive

Extensions

- Add images of events to the date's cell. Use clipart or Google images. Resize to fit. (see sample below on December 24th)

Troubleshooting Tips

- *I'm typing and my text doesn't show (Is there an 'A' or '...' under the cell? That's the overflow code, meaning there's more text than fits in the allowed space. Make the font size smaller or abbreviate your information.)*

Subject #2: Composition and Communication

Project #24: A Holiday Newsletter in Publisher. Have students collaborate on a newsletter for a classroom unit of inquiry or a theme (colonies, animals, etc.). Pick a template. Add text and pictures. Pay attention to layout details. Allow several class periods to complete

Higher-order thinking skills	Technology-specific:	Subject Area/ Learning-specific	Standard: ISTE
Analyzing, organizing parts	*Using templates, the three c's, editing templates, layout*	*Grammar and spelling, collaborative skills*	*6a-d*

Grade level: 5-8
Prior knowledge: Introduction to Publisher, Project 21, 22, 23 (card, flier, calendar)
Time required: 45 minutes, 2 sessions (prep time outside of class)
Software required: Publisher (or your class DTP tool)
Vocabulary: DTP, place saver, template, overflow, design gallery, link, embedded, master, stock photos, hyperbole,

Lesson Description

- Publisher is one of many desktop publishing (DTP) programs used to create brochures, magazines, newsletters—and more—with easy-to-use, easy-to-personalize templates.
- While its strength for educators is often seen as magazines and trifold brochures, newsletters offer collaborative and active learning experiences for students unavailable with other projects. They provide an engaging, student-focused culture in the classroom, while encouraging positive interdependence as well as individual accountability for the success of the project.
- Newsletters are best completed in groups to promote collaborative research and inquiry-based learning, as students
- The program includes a broad selection of templates with stock items—columns, headings, titles, table of contents, design elements—arranged in attractive layouts. By using these stock place savers, students need only:
- Insert stories and titles
- Add relevant pictures
- Complete the Table of Contents

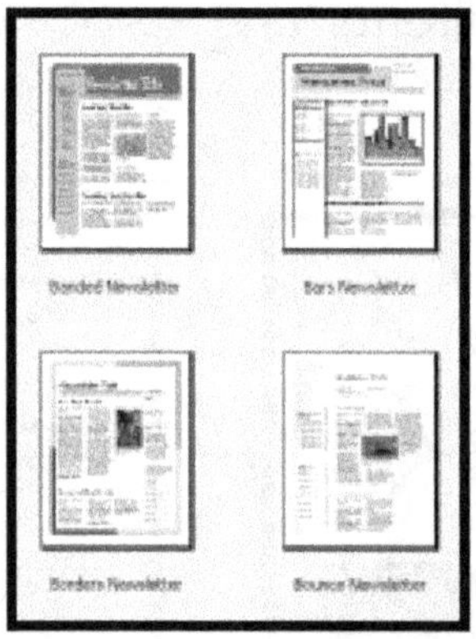

- This is an advanced project, using all Publisher elements acquired from Projects 21-23. It can be adapted to holidays, class events, back-to-school, or to share summer plans.
- If this is their first newsletter, students should be encouraged to keep it simple by limiting stories to the space allotted and use the template's embedded formatting.

Computer Activity

Note: Other DTP tools, like Canva, can be used if you don't have Publisher.

- Students should come to class with two stories for a one page newsletter or five stories for two pages. These should be an interdisciplinary collection gathered from many sources. These can support classroom discussion on a topic (i.e., California Missions) or other themes.

- Select 'Newsletters'. Click the template you like. From the right hand column, adjust 'Font Schemes' and 'Color Schemes'. Click 'create'.
- Delete unnecessary pages from left sidebar so you have only two or four (or whatever number you need).
- Add newsletter title. Pick something splashy and significant for your group that describes the newsletter's purpose. As you type in, the font size is adjusted to fit the length. Don't try to do this yourself.

- Add a title for 'Lead Story' by clicking in the words and editing for your title. Do the same with the 'Secondary Story'. These should be a few words to describe what's in the story and motivate the audience to read on. Hyperbole is fine if it's accurate.

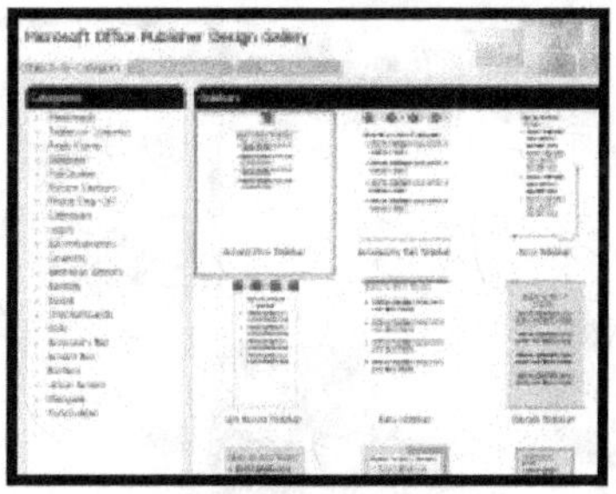

- Each article will have text and one picture.
- Enter articles one of three ways:

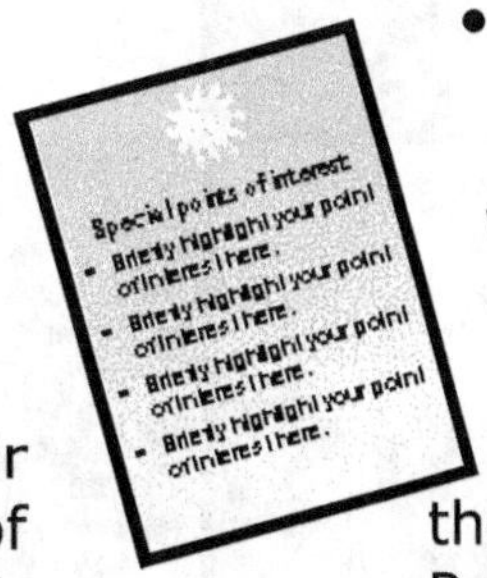

  - o Each student adds their article into a saved copy of the group's newsletter (open it on their computer, add info and save-as under their name. Then, copy their columns and paste into master)
  - o Each student adds their article into the master one at a time (during lunch, before/after school, from home if they have Publisher).
  - o The group appoints a scribe (probably the fastest typist).

Remind students to keep text within the allotted column space. If they exhaust their story notes, add pictures. Resize the images to fill all white space. A full page gives the impression of busy, active, authentic.

- Replace the template's stock photos with pictures pertinent to your story using clipart or Google images. Students can insert-picture or copy-paste from the internet.
- After all stories and pictures have been added, students might still have white space remaining. To fill this, Publisher offers multiple choices in the Design Gallery:
  - sidebars and pull quotes to highlight important information (see inset)
  - interactive items such as reply forms, phone tear offs, etc. (see inset)

When inserted, objects are recolored to match the scheme.

- You'll probably notice the story automatically flows into the next column. This is because Publisher links related columns . You can break that link with the ribbon  tool and add an unlinked column.
- Find the text box entitled 'Inside This Issue' (see inset). Put story titles and page numbers into the rows provided. Delete extra rows. Enlarge box to fill any white space.

- Find the text box entitled 'Special Points of Interest' (see inset). Fill this with whatever would be appealing to your audience—holiday gifts, vacations spots, New Year's resolutions. This box will attract readers' attention so make it splashy.
- Check grammar and spelling.

Extensions

- Adapt column lengths for longer or shorter stories by dragging handles at bottom or top of column. Be sure the entire column shows and there are no text overflows (an 'A' at the bottom of the column).
- Make a newsletter to go along with a classroom unit (see example below)
- Email the newsletter to classmates rather than print. The colors will be more vibrant and it won't get lost.

Troubleshooting Tips

- *I'm typing but nothing shows (Is there an 'A' under your column? That's the overflow warning—your column's too small. Resize the column or write less!)*
- *How do I delete a page? (Right-click tab and select 'delete'.)*

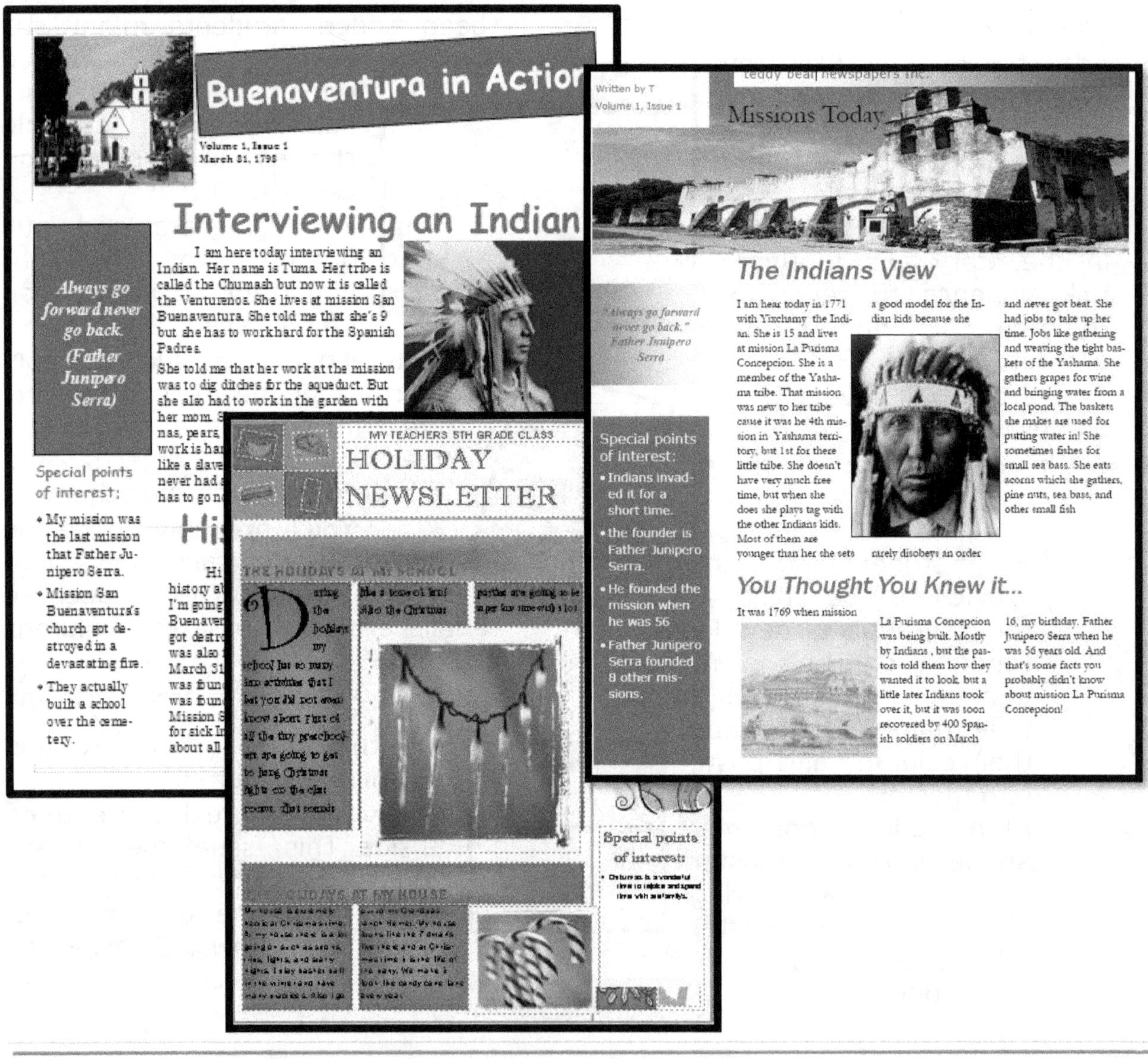

Subject #2: Composition and Communication

Project #25: Four-sentence story in KidPix Draw four pictures on different themes, using four different KidPix tools. Assign topics (me, my family, etc.) or use topics from class inquiry. Each slide has a picture and title. Students show these at Open House or a parent night using Windows slideshow (some can do without assistance)

Higher-order thinking skills	Technology-specific:	Subject Area/ Learning-specific	Standard: ISTE
Creating, comprehension, organizing	*Adding/editing text, using tools/toolbars*	*Story-telling, grammar, spelling, composition*	*6a, 6d*

Grade level: K, 1
Prior knowledge: Project 1/2 (KidPix Basx I/II)
Time required: 30 minutes, 8 sessions (2 for each drawing)
Software required: KidPix (or your class art tool)
Vocabulary: text, grammar, animation, slideshow, PowerPoint, undo, toolbar

Lesson Description

- This is a favorite at my school. Students proudly share a year's worth of tech achievements.
- When students complete their four projects, you as the teacher meld them into a slideshow for parents.

Computer Activity

Note: If you don't have KidPix, use the school drawing program.

- Allow two classes for each drawing, one to practice and one to perfect it.
- Kindergarten writes a phrase for each picture; first grade writes a full sentence using the text tool font size 48, any font, any color (see following pages). Each picture uses a different skill as follows:
    - #1: (sample on next page is M is for Me) Use the thick pencil tool (no chalk, magic marker or crayon) so it shows up in the slideshow. Use 5 colors.
    - #2: (sample on next page is My Family) Use the paint brush—five colors and a different brush for each family member.
    - #3: (sample on next page is My House) Use the paint brush 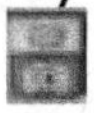 wacky tool building tools.
    - #4: Kindergarten (sample is My Neighborhood) Use the pencil tool to draw a street and the paint bucket fill tool (#3)  to add grass, clouds, streets, etc.
    - #4: 1st Grade—Permit use of stamps on one picture.
- These skills have been practiced throughout the year so encourage students to work independently.
- Check for grammar and spelling.
- Use a slideshow to turn student work into a celebration of their achievement. Add fun music to the background.

Extensions

- Email the slideshow to parents.

Troubleshooting Tips

- *I goofed and the Oops guy*  *couldn't undo it! (Start over. That's why you practice one week and draw the next.)*

Left column—Kindergarten KidPix drawings. Right column shows drawings in slideshow program.

Left column: 1st grade KidPix drawings. Right column : drawings in a slideshow program.

Subject #2: Composition and Communication

Project #26: Four-sentence Story—Advanced—in KidPix, PowerPoint. Write and illustrate a story using the characteristics of fiction and put the story into a slideshow. Through this exercise, students learn the PowerPoint basics (inserting pictures and text, animation, transition, inserting clipart, auto-advance, sound), skills that are reinforced in third and fourth grade. By fifth grade, they're autonomous. Students present their slideshow to practice the unique skills of presentations using PowerPoint

Higher-order thinking skills	Technology-specific:	Subject Area/ Learning-specific	Standard: ISTE
Creating, organizing comprehension,	*Adding/editing text, using tools/toolbars*	*Story-telling, grammar, spelling, composition*	*6a, 6d*

Grade level: 2-4
Prior knowledge: PowerPoint basics; Project 1/2; Project 25
Time required: 30 minutes for each drawing and story element
Software required: KidPix, PowerPoint (or your class art and presentation tools)
Vocabulary: plot, character, animations, GIFs, auto-advance, transitions

Lesson Description

- This is a favorite at my school as students share what they learned through the year with parents.
- This project reinforces classroom introduction to writing stories.
- This project is the first of three years of projects to teach students PowerPoint. By fifth grade, they can create a slideshow on their own.

Computer Activity

Note: No KidPix? Use your school drawing program.

- Show slideshows from last year.
- Each sentence covers an important fiction trait—character, plot, setting, climax/resolution. Discuss these with students.
- Write a four-sentence story, font 36, any font/color:
    - #1: Introduce themselves with a unique descriptor. Illustrate with pencil tool and five colors.
    - #2: Tell where they live with a unique descriptor of the house. Illustrate with the paint brush wacky tool (building tools). See next page for sample.
    - #3: What does the student wish? Illustrate with paint brush tool.
    - #4: How does student accomplish their wish? Illustrate with background tool, paint brush and up to five stamps/stickers.
- Check for grammar and spelling.
- When finished, introduce students to PowerPoint basics and guide them through turning their work into a slideshow with transitions, animation, transitions, clipart, movies (kids love the moving pictures), unique backgrounds.

Extensions

- Write more than one sentence per picture

Troubleshooting Tips

- *Oops guy couldn't undo! (Start over. That's why you practice one week and draw the next.)*
- *Trouble getting started (Model your story after a fairy tale)*

Left column shows the KidPix drawings done by students. The right column shows drawings imported into slideshow.

Subject #2: Composition and Communication

Project #27: Online Blogs: Blogs are a revolutionary method to give all students an equal voice in conversations. Create a classroom blog to continue classroom discussions after class. Show students how to interact on it, answer questions, add their ideas. Include pictures, student schedule, location of your wiki and more

Higher-order thinking skills	Technology-specific	Subject Area/ Learning-specific	Standard: ISTE
Creating, generating, integrating	*Internet skills, keyboarding*	*Spelling, grammar, composition, critical thinking*	*6a-d*

Grade level: 5-8
Prior knowledge: Project 99 and 100—from Book II of this collection
Time required: 10 minutes a week
Software required: internet
Vocabulary: blog, wiki, netiquette, rss feed, blog roll, avatar, posts, virtual

Lesson Description

- Studies show 32 million people read blogs daily. 32 million people—reading? Conventional wisdom declared reading had been replaced with sound bites and YouTube videos. What's going on?
- Let's start with what a bog is. It's a web log—like a diary or journal, but internet based. No software to install or keep up to date. No IT glitches. Just a web browser, you and your class. A blogger posts a topic and instantly anyone can respond—in real time—with thoughts, opinions, disagreements, research, whatever comes to mind.

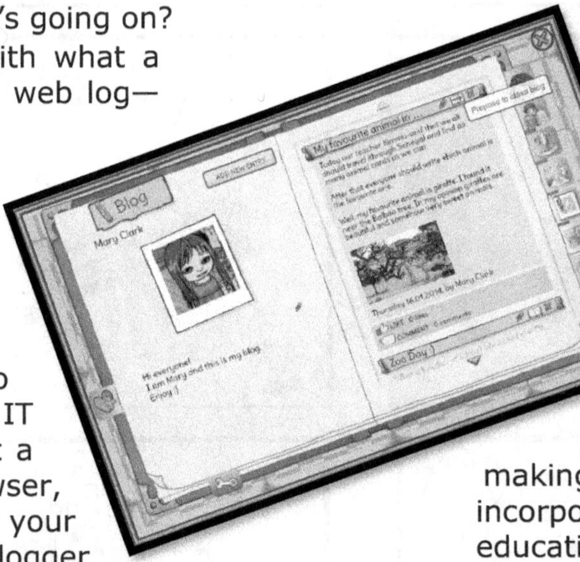

- Blogs have spread like wild fire through not just the virtual world but sticks-and-bricks schools, businesses, and the entire Web 2.0 generation. With a blog, you not only can host a discussion, but post resources and lesson plans for students. It encourages critical thinking with authentic questions in a collaborative learning environment that is non-threatening and student-centered. Students who won't talk in class often participate in a blog.
- The case for blogging in schools is clear. They bolster technology skills, attract a wider audience than traditional reading venues, improve student writing skills by making writing fun and hip, incorporate discovery into education, and draw learners into self-guided discussions with each other. It requires critical thinking of participants, and more importantly, gives ownership of content to students.
- What should you include as blog posts?

- Use them for journaling, reflection, research, analysis, sharing, debating, or open forums
- Post daily class activities with pictures and notes, reminders of quizzes, homework due, websites and links of interest to students and parents

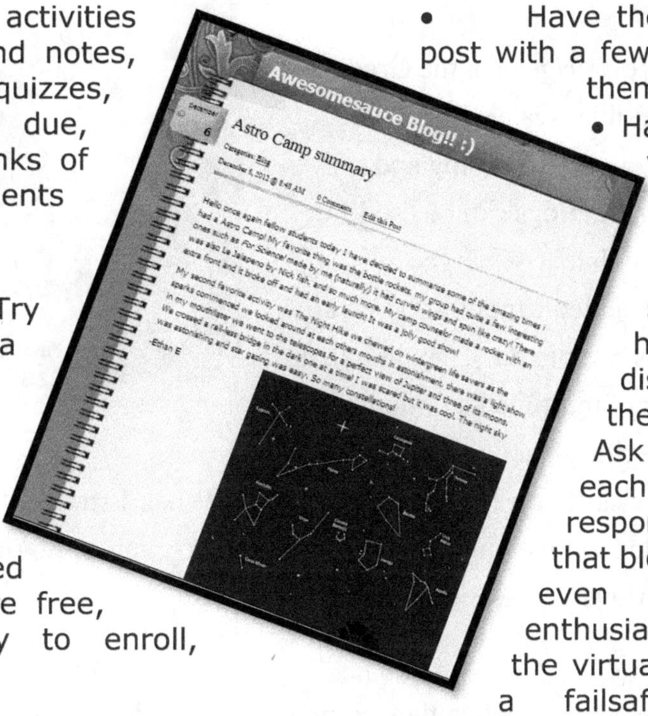

- Still pondering? Try this website for a long list of educators who already blog.

Computer Activity

- Get yourself signed up! Many blogs are free, customizable, easy to enroll, easier to use. Try:
    - *Kidblog*
    - *Edublogs*

Once you're up and running, have students read your blog. Make sure you have at least a month's worth of entries so students can view the progression of ideas, the widgets, the blog roll, and more.

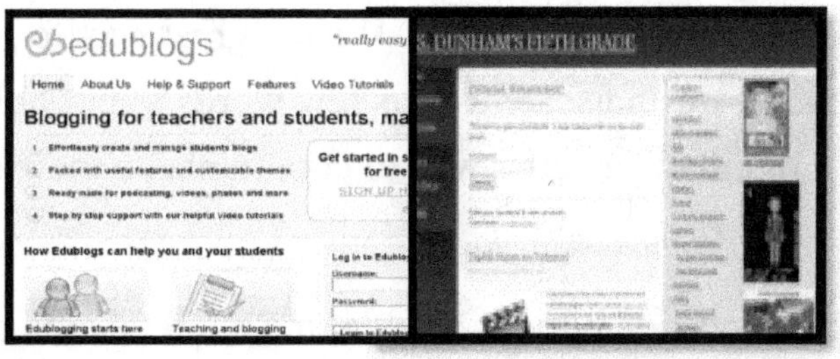

- Next, encourage them to select several of your entries and make comments.
- Respond to student comments! Nothing is worse than talking to a void.
- When (older) students set up their blog, make sure they select a meaningful name as it will often become part of their address.
    - Have them create a first post with a few sentences about themselves.
    - Have them email you the blog's name.
    - Pick topics to get them started, maybe have students discuss a book they're all reading. Ask them to read each other's blogs and respond. You may find that blog reading makes even the nonreaders enthusiastic about turning the virtual page. It is also a failsafe method of ensuring all students are heard, all ideas aired.

Extensions

- Did we mention blogs are usually free? See Project 101 for more sites.
- When students go on a field trip, have them blog their thoughts. If it's an overnighter, have them do this from the road.

Troubleshooting Tips

- *How do I do this? (Take a deep breath. You can do it. One step at a time...)*

7–no 10, wait 12–OK, 13 Skills I Teach With Blogging

Blogging has become *de rigeur* in the Grade 3-8 classroom. It is flexible, scalable, and encourages diversity in both learning and teaching. Handled right, blogs can be used for pretty much any need that arises in the classroom. It has the added benefit of being an activity that students want to do. They like that it's online, with lots of multimedia options, and a focus not on writing but communication. I decided to track the skills I teach through blogging. When I started, I had seven, but as I continued, it exploded to this long list that I'm adding to even as I write this post. Read through these, tell me other ways you use it in your class:

Collaboration

Students collaborate on blogs when they comment on the ideas of others. They can also take it a step further by collaborating on the blog itself. Be co-owners of the blog, themed to a particular topic, and work together to fulfill goals.

Developing a profile

Blog profiles must be pithy, concise, and clear. What a great way for students to think through what makes them who they are and share it in as few words as possible. I am constantly reworking my own as I figure out a better way to communicate the gist of who I am.

Differentiation

There are so many communication options in blogging–well beyond the stalwart written word:

- *text*
- *images*
- *videos*
- *clipart*
- *gifs*
- *how-to whiteboard videos*
- *embeds*
- *screenshots*
- *links*

Students learn to select the strategy that best suits their purpose and audience, as they seek to connect with all types of learners. It matters less what they use than that it is the right tool for the purpose. That's differentiation.

Digital footprints

Students want to blog because it puts them online, but before they begin, they must understand the concept of 'digital footprint'. With that as the entry ticket to getting online, they listen and then practice with every post they publish. *Listen, try, edit, try again, edit again*–they come to understand the right way to do online communication.

Embedding information

This is always a tricky concept for students. Maybe it's because it tiptoes through html and coding–still considered by many as something they can't do. Blogs provide an opportunity to embed so many fun webtools–Wordles, Animotos, Tagxedos, timelines–that students will want to figure out this geeky skill. That's the first step to learning: Wanting to do it. Once desire is kindled, students will slog through the nerdy stuff to embed a fun Voki–and discover it's not so bad. Which means they'll do it more often.

Keyboarding skills

Though blogs use many media, their essence remains text. Students must be good at keyboarding to efficiently use blogs. That's a good thing.

Perspective-taking

Because blogs are published to the world, students will quickly realize that they are better received if the student shows an understanding of life outside their personal bubble. Their opinions and attitudes are honed by their life and circumstances. Writing a post that reflects that perspective while accepting others have not walked in their shoes is powerful. As it is with commenting on others' posts. This is essential to good blogging. Students who want to blog will accept this requirement, and eventually own it.

Protect Privacy

Avatars are a great way to begin the conversation about online privacy. Students love making these quirky, creative images of how they see themselves. A perfect spot to use them that continues the discussion is the blog profile.

Reflection

The root of blogging is journaling. Back in the day, it was a way to share daily thoughts. It's grown up since then, but remains a personal perspective on topics, issues, discussions (with the critical addition of evidence and relevance–features that exploded blogging's popularity). Reflection is a task at the core of many lesson plans. It is well-delivered with blogs.

Sharing/collaborating

Kids want to put their entire lives online. After they understand concepts of privacy and safe surfing, blogs provide a way to share ideas, collaborate through posts and comments–even co-own a themed blog.

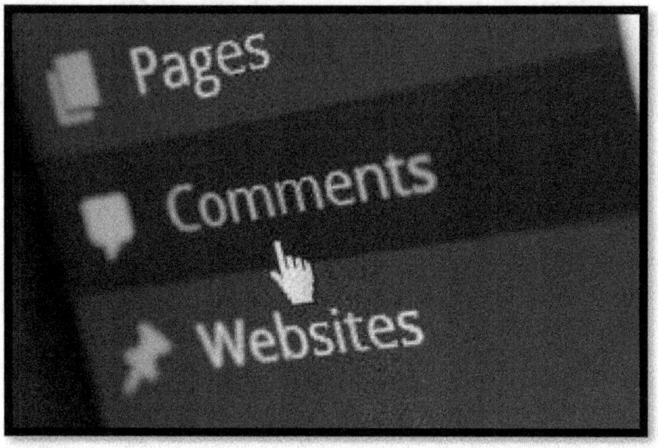

Spelling

Blogs include annoying red lines that tell you something is misspelled. It used to be just word processing programs had them, but now, they're everywhere. It takes seconds to correct spelling but does wonders for an online presence that will follow students through high school, college, and beyond.

Writing skills

Blogs don't hone all writing skills, just the cogent, pithy presentation of ideas in 300-1000 words. Most students are happy with that mitigated limit. They'll write-review-edit-rewrite and make a better post.

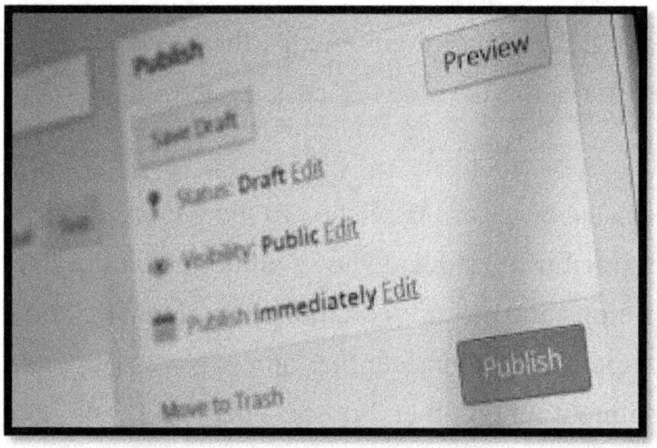

Adding comments to classmates' blogs is more writing practice. Students must stay on topic, provide evidence from the post they're commenting on, understand the perspective of the writer, understand their position enough that the commenter can offer his/her thoughts on that, and make the response quick and purposeful. That's a lot of learning in a few sentences.

Blogging Platforms

There are many blogging platforms. What works best for you will depend upon the age of your students and their needs.

Subject #2: Composition and Communication

Project #28: My Storybook—in Publisher. Create a ten-sentence illustrated story using characters, setting, plot, rising action, climax and resolution. Have one sentence per page with a picture to communicate the idea. Include a cover, ending page, and About the Author. Use this lesson to teach students how to use Publisher's design gallery and an authentic assessment/review of classroom inquiry into writing pedagogy.

Higher-order thinking skills	Technology-specific:	Subject Area/ Learning-specific	Standard: ISTE
Creating, organizing comprehension,	*Adding/editing text, using tools/toolbars*	*Story-telling, grammar, spelling, composition*	*4a, 4b, 6a, 6b*

Grade level: 3-7
Prior knowledge: Introduction to Publisher; Project 21, 22, 23 (card, flier, calendar); comfort level with keyboarding skills
Time required: 45 minutes, six sessions
Software required: Publisher (or your class DTP tool)
Vocabulary: template, populate, font, rubric, grammar, TuxPaint

Lesson Description

- Publisher is one of many desktop publishing (DTP) programs used to create brochures, magazines, storybooks—and more—with easy-to-use, easy-to-personalize templates.
- While its strength for educators is often seen as magazines and trifold brochures, a storybook is an engaging project that allows students to focus on their personal strengths—art or words—with this interdisciplinary array of skills.

- A storybook allows both writers and artists to succeed, and each to find value in the other.
- If this is their first illustrated story, students should be encouraged to keep it simple. Make sentences clear, but descriptive. Make pictures themed to a character or action.

Computer Activity

Note: If you don't have Publisher, use your school's DTP program.

- Discuss writing strategies with students. Explain the traits of fiction—character, plot, setting, climax/ resolution. Chat about these before students write their story.
- Have them review their ten sentences with you prior to beginning the project. Are there any grammar or spelling errors? Who is the main character? What is the plot? The setting? The climax and resolution?
- Open Publisher. Have them pick the Quick Publication layout. Adjust colors and fonts using Color and Font Schemes (as done in #22).

- Add the story title in place of 'Heading'. Add their name and teacher in place of 'Subheading'.

- Use KidPix, Paint, or TuxPaint to draw a picture that illustrates the story's theme (or the main character, or the plot). Export as a .jpg (with teacher assistance if needed). Insert it in place of the stock photo on the cover.
- Add eleven pages to the project. They'll populate in the left sidebar. If necessary, select the layout with a text box and an image.

- Add a border to each page from Insert-borders. Keep the border consistent on all pages.
- Add one sentence per page—centered, font size 48, any font, any color. (See sample below.)
- Add a picture that goes with the text at the top of each page. These can be drawn in KidPix, Paint, TuxPaint, or inserted from clip art or Google images. Skip the last page. We'll do this one differently (see sample).
- Resize the picture and text on pages 2-11 to fill the page. Don't leave any white space.
- Copy-paste the cover picture to the last page. Bring up the Picture Format dialogue box (right click or use keyboard right-click key) and change the image from 'automatic' to 'washout'.
- Resize so it fills the page. Layer it behind using the ribbon's layer tool
- Add 'The End' using WordArt.
- Check for grammar and spelling.
- Have students take responsibility for their learning by completing the rubric (see next page) to be sure they've followed all instructions.

Extensions

- Vary the layout of picture/text box to student taste.
- Record the story for younger children.
- Use the 10-sentence story (prior to creating the storybook) in conjunction with Project 32: Color My Grammar to work out grammar problems.

Troubleshooting Tips

- *I can't find my story! (Did you back it up to your flash drive? Is it saved in 'My Documents rather than the network folder?)*

Storybook Grading Rubric

Creator: ____________________

Teacher: ____________________

Date: ____________________

1. Title Page includes	______
a. Story title in large font	______
b. Your name in smaller font	______
c. KidPix Picture related to topic	______
2. Each Story Page includes	______
a. Border	______
b. Picture appropriate for story	______
c. Spell-check	______
d. Page filled (text/pictures)	______
3. Provide evidence that you	______
a. Established a situation	______
b. Introduced characters	______
c. Organized event to unfold naturally	______
d. Used dialogue to develop events	______
e. Used description to develop events	______
f. Used transitional words to manage sequence	______
g. Used concrete words to convey events	______
h. Used sensory details to convey events	______
i. Concluded story based on narrated events.	______
4. About the Author includes	______
a. A few points about yourself	______
b. Border	______
5. The End Page has	______
a. The End in WordArt	______
b. Watermark of cover	______
6. Overall Professional Look	______

Subject #2: Composition and Communication

Project #29: All About Me—in PowerPoint. Have students create a slideshow to communicate using multiple forms of media. Include a table of contents for olders. Use this project to reinforce the PowerPoint basics learned in 2nd grade—adding slides/text/pictures, animation, transitions, clipart, internet pictures, and auto-advance. Have each student present their slideshow to practice the unique skills of presentations using PowerPoint

Higher-order thinking skills	Technology-specific:	Subject Area/ Learning-specific	Standard: ISTE
Creating, organizing comprehension,	*Adding/editing text, using tools/toolbars*	*Story-telling, grammar, spelling, composition*	*4a, 4b, 6a, 6b*

Grade level: 3-4
Prior knowledge: Introduction to PowerPoint, Project 26: Four-slide story
Time required: 30 minutes, 5 sessions
Software required: PowerPoint (or your class presentation tool)
Vocabulary: slides, transitions, animations, animated GIFs, place holders,

Lesson Description

- In 1995, a UC Davis study found that eighty-five percent of people fear public speaking. It hasn't changed in fifteen years. Talking in front of an audience is difficult and intimidating, but when PowerPoint is used, the focal point becomes the slideshow instead of the speaker.

- Today, Microsoft estimates that 30 million PowerPoint presentations are created a day. In many schools, it is the new chalkboard.
- What is this behemoth of the public speaking world? It's software with a bulleted interface that keeps the audience focused on what's important, no matter the skills of the speaker, with colors and sounds that keep the audience entranced no matter how boring the presenter.

Computer Activity

Note: If you don't have PowerPoint, use your school's slideshow program.

- Review PowerPoint's layout and tools (Students should have completed Project #26).
- Show students *All About Me* slideshows from last year's students. This will motivate them, challenge them and take the fear of the unknown out of this new project.
- Open PowerPoint. Add title, *All About Me*. Add student name and teacher where it says, 'Click to add subtitle'.
- Add 9 slides with the new slide  tool (click the icon, not the words, to get the slide layout shown in the inset).

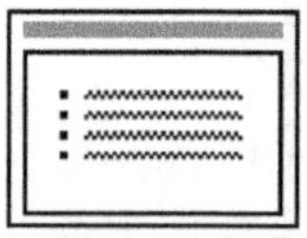

- Slide 2: Add title, 'Table of Contents' and bullet list of items per the list on next page.

- Slides 3-9: Add titles per Table of Contents. Backspace to delete the bullet list in the text place saver. Add a sentence about the topic's favorite.
- Slide 10: Add title, 'About the Author'. Have students use text area to discuss themselves.
- Accept all defaults for text. If you've done this correctly, the titles on all slides will be the same font, color and size. If not, take time now to make text consistent across all titles and sentences.

- Click Design (menu item) and select a theme. This will add a background to each slide. Try a few before deciding. Or, add a unique background to each slide by right-clicking on the background and selecting 'apply to selected slide'.
- Add a picture from clip art or Google images to each slide. Make sure it matches the slide's topic (i.e., the 'Favorite Sport' slide should not have a picture of ice cream).
- Add a movie (i.e., an animated GIF) to each slide. These are found under Insert-movies. Or, the teacher can collect a file folder of GIFs that deal with favorites and show students how to drill down to that network file.

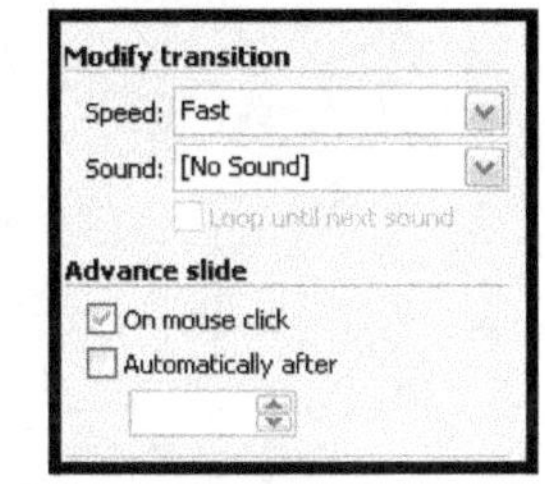

- To see the movie move, click Shift+F5 (this plays slideshow from current slide).
- Add transitions between slides with the menu item, 'Transitions'. Once you select it, it's on the slide. While in the 'transition' screen, select 'automatically after' to advance slide without pushing the spacebar or mouse button. Five seconds is usually long enough between slides.
- Animate text by selecting the menu item, 'Animation' and selecting the theme you like. As with transitions, once you pick it, it's on the slide.
- Check sample slide below to see the four points required on each slide. Have students take responsibility for their learning by completing rubrics before scheduling presentations. Remember grammar and spelling.
- During the presentation, follow guidelines on Presentation rubric.

Extensions

- Advanced students can customize backgrounds, add sounds, a custom track of music, and interactive hyperlinks to the table of contents
- Visit my blog for an extensive list of animated GIFs to use with this project.
- Need to tie into classroom inquiry? See the next pages for an example of a project that does that. You can customize it to your needs.

Troubleshooting Tips

- *Every time I change the background for one, it changes all of them (Be sure to right-click and select 'current slide').*

SLIDESHOW GRADING RUBRIC

*Name*____________________ *Teacher*__________________

Here's a list of skills required in your project. Check off those that you've included. Then, add those you've missed. Parentheses indicates extra credit. When you're done, turn in the rubric and I'll grade your project.

1.	Title slide	__________
2.	About the Author slide	__________
3.	Table of Contents	__________
4.	Each slide has title	__________
5.	Each slide has sentence of favorite	__________
6.	Each slide has picture	__________
7.	Each slide has GIF	__________
8.	Fonts consistent on all slides	__________
9.	Pictures match topic on slide	__________
10.	No spelling/grammar errors	__________
11.	5 animations	__________
12.	5 transitions	__________
13.	Slides auto-advance	__________

SLIDESHOW PRESENTATION

Name ____________________

Teacher ____________________

Date ____________________

Face audience ____________________

Talk to audience ____________________

Introduce yourself ____________________

Introduce your topic ____________________

Speak loudly and clearly ____________________

No 'umms', slang, or stuttering ____________________

Answer questions ____________________

Slide show progresses smoothly ____________________

Understood topic ____________________

Need a slideshow project tied to a classroom unit? Try this:

3rd Grade Slideshow Project: Government

Your name:____________________________________

Your teacher:____________________________________

Slide 1: Cover

Slide 2: Table of Contents

Slide 3: Why do people need government/What does government do:

1. ____________________________________
2. ____________________________________
3. ____________________________________

Slide 4: Features of a democracy:

1. ____________________________________
2. ____________________________________
3. ____________________________________

Slide 5: Features of a monarchy:

1. ____________________________________
2. ____________________________________
3. ____________________________________

Slide 6: Features of a dictatorship:

1. ______________________________
2. ______________________________
3. ______________________________

Slide 7: Three branches of US government:

1. ______________________________
2. ______________________________
3. ______________________________

Slide 8: About the Author

1. Your name and family names
2. Where you live
3. Your favorite book
4. Your goal for life
5. Anything else we should know about you

Samples

Take M
By Torrey J
Ms. Hoffm
GOVERNMENTS
BY STUDENTS FOR TEACHER
Features of a Dem
The definition of Democracy is a government by
An example of a democracy is America
A feature of Democracy is freedom
ment

SLIDESHOW GRADING RUBRIC

"Take Me To Your Leader"

Third Grade

*Name*____________________ *Teacher*__________________

Here's a list of required skills in your PowerPoint project. Check off those that you've included. Then, add those that you've missed. When you're done, turn in the grading rubric and I'll grade your project.

1. Title slide ________________
2. About the Author slide ________________
3. Table of Contents ________________
4. Each slide has title ________________
5. Each slide has bullets from storyboard ________________
6. Each slide has picture ________________
7. Each slide has movie (GIF) ________________
8. No spelling/grammar errors ________________
9. 5 animations ________________
10. 5 transitions ________________
11. 5 sounds ________________
12. Slides auto-advance ________________
13. Class presentation ________________
    a. Face audience ________________
    b. Talk to audience ________________
    c. Introduce yourself and topic ________________
    d. Speak loud enough ________________
    e. No 'umms' or stuttering ________________
14. (Custom background) ________________
15. (Custom animation) ________________

Subject #2: Composition and Communication

Project #30: A Cover Page in Publisher . Use the Quick Publication template to make a fast cover page for a report, project, etc., that supports a unit of inquiry in the classroom. Pay attention to layout, grammar, spelling, design

Higher-order thinking skills	Technology-specific:	Subject Area/ Learning-specific	Standard: ISTE
Applying, Creating, Organizing	*Use of templates, desktop publishing,*	*Composition, grammar, spelling,*	*6a-d*

Grade level: 3-7
Prior knowledge: Introduction to Publisher, Project 22: Holiday Flier
Time required: 15 minutes
Software required: MS Publisher (or your class DTP tool)
Vocabulary: template, placeholders, DTP, screen, font, schemes

Lesson Description

- Publisher is desktop publishing (DTP) software for creating brochures, magazines—and more—with easy-to-use, easy-to-personalize templates.
- Cover pages are a great way to learn Publisher. They're simple to make, exciting for project-oriented students, and a fulfilling introduction to a robust, sometimes challenging program.
- The cover page template has:
  - A stock picture, to be replaced with a personalized one
  - A place saver for report title
  - A second place saver for student name

Computer Activity

Note: If you don't have Publisher, use your school's DTP program.

- Open Publisher. Select 'Quick Publications'. Scroll through the templates and select one.
- Adjust color/font schemes as desired in right column. Click 'create'.
- Take a quick tour of the main screen:
  - Cover in the center.
  - One page on left
  - Ribbon with tools at top.
- Turn student attention to the template in middle of screen.
- 'Heading': Click this word and add the report title. Don't worry about size. It'll adjust as needed.
- 'Sub-heading': Click and add student name and teacher. Again, font size adjusts to fit.
- Picture: Delete the stock picture and add one from clipart or Google images that complements the topic.
- Check grammar and spelling. Save to network folder and flash drive

Extensions

- Adjust font and color separate from predesigned schemes
- Be sure all internet pictures used are royalty-free.

Troubleshooting Tips

- *The font is too big. (Don't worry. It resizes as you type. Everything will fit.)*
- *I found a picture on the internet and it doesn't work right on the template. (Did you use the thumbnail instead of the full-size image? Click the thumbnail image once and again for the full-size image.)*

Samples

Subject #2: Composition and Communication

Project #31: A Title Page and Cover Page in Word. Create a title page and cover page using MS Word. This is more difficult than #30 (cover page using Publisher) so allow more time. Have students include text and picture as well as a border

Higher-order thinking skills	Technology-specific	Subject Area/ Learning-specific	Standard: ISTE
Applying, Creating, Organizing	*Use of templates, desktop publishing,*	*Composition, grammar, spelling,*	*4a, 6a, 6b*

Grade level: 3-7
Prior knowledge: Introduction to Word
Time required: Title page: 10 minutes; Cover page: 20 minutes
Software required: MS Word (or your class word processing tool)
Vocabulary: washout, watermark, vertically centered, dialogue box, border, alignment, double-space, format

Lesson Description

- Create a cover page and a title page to support classroom inquiry into a topic.
- Make sure students understand the differences

Computer Activity

Note: If you don't have Word, use your school's word processing program.

- Open MS Word. Use font size 36, centered, Times New Roman or Arial.
- For Title Page, select triple-space from the ribbon.
- Type the report name, teacher, student name and date on separate lines (see top inset).
- Click 'page layout', 'paragraph' on ribbon. Next, select 'center' under 'General Alignment' to center words vertically on page.
- Check grammar and spelling.
- For Cover Page, undo the vertical centering. You'll need the room at the bottom of the page for a picture.

- Go to Google images. Search for a picture of your project. Go to full size image; copy.
- Paste the picture under text (see inset). Use center alignment on the ribbon to center.
- Now, copy the picture and paste it onto the page (anywhere because we will be formatting it)

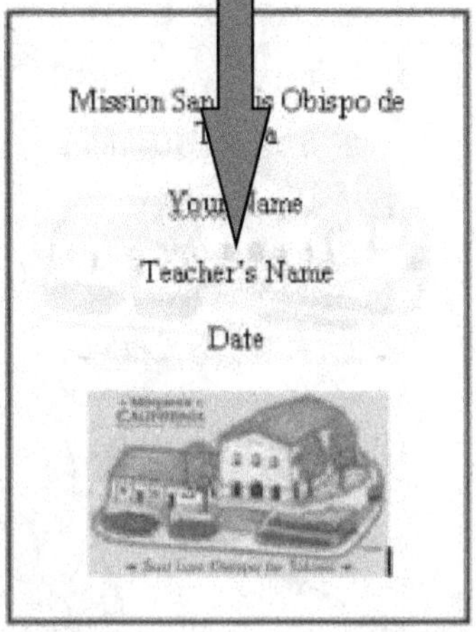

- Right-click the picture to bring up the picture formatting dialogue box. Go to 'Layout' tab and change wrap to 'behind'. Go to 'Picture' tab and change picture to 'washout' (from automatic)
- Resize image to fill page
- Add a line border, any color or thickness, but no art borders. Save

Extensions

- Use a different picture for washout.

Troubleshooting Tips

- *The picture covers my text (Did you change it to 'watermark'? Did you change 'wrap' to 'behind'?)*

Subject #2: Composition and Communication

Project #32: Color my Grammar (in MS Word). Students type several sentences in MS Word. Use the font color palette to label parts of speech, i.e., blue for subject, red for verb. You can use sentences from a book they're reading in class, spelling words they're working on, or a teacher hand-out. Makes grammar fun.

Higher-order thinking skills	Technology-specific:	Subject Area/ Learning-specific	Standard: ISTE
Analyzing, understanding, evaluating	*Tools and toolbars,*	*grammar*	*3a, 5b*

Grade level: 3-8
Prior knowledge: Introduction to MS Word, comfort-level with keyboarding
Time required: 30 minutes
Software required: MS Word (or your class word processing tool)
Vocabulary: noun, verb, adjective, adverb, pronoun, conjunction, prepositional phrase

Lesson Description

- This is a fun way for students to recognize parts of speech.
- Traditional grammar classifies words into eight categories. You can use as many or as few as works for your grammar program.
- You can use a paragraph from a textbook, from fiction they're reading in class, or one of their choice.

Computer Activity

Note: If you don't have Word, use your school's word processing program.

- Open Word. Students type a paragraph you've selected. Use font size 18.
- Have them mark parts of speech with the highlighter tool ( ) according to the legend on the next page.
- Have students work in pairs and check each other's work.
- When finished, have them add a legend with each color and what it stands for at the bottom
- Print; save to student network folder; save-as to flash drive as a back-up

Extensions

- Turn this around. Pass out a sheet where you have highlighted words in colors and have students identify what part of speech they are. For example, what are the grey words on the next page?

Troubleshooting Tips

- *I can't get the highlighter to work (two ways: 1) double-click the word and select the color from the highlighter, or, 2) select the highlighter color and then paint over the word.*
- *My document disappeared (check the taskbar. Did it fall asleep?)*

Type several sentences in MS Word. Use the font color palette and clearly label parts of speech—yellow for noun, green for verb, red for adjective, blue for adverb, pink for pronoun, and purple for prepositional phrases. You can carefully use sentences from a book you are reading in class, or spelling words you are working on.

_______ = *noun*

_______ = *verb*

_______ = *adjective*

_______ = *adverb*

_______ = *pronoun*

_______ = *prepositional phrases*

Subject #2: Composition and Communication

Project #33: Grow Your Story Using Word Provide a first- or second-grade version of a story (limited character development, no scenery, no sensory input). Ask students to engage their critical thinking skills; determine why a story sounds amateurish and morph it to one sophisticated enough for the upper grades by adding descriptions, setting details, sensory details, characterization.

Higher-order thinking skills	Technology-specific:	Subject Area/ Learning-specific	Standard: ISTE
Understanding information, generating ideas	*Keyboarding, editing text, use of tools and toolbars*	*Spelling, grammar, composition*	*1.c, 1d*

Grade level: 3-6
Prior knowledge: Introduction to MS Word, comfort-level with keyboarding
Time required: 20 minutes
Software required: MS Word (or your class word processing tool)
Vocabulary: doc, sensory, scenery, plot, character, hook, proof read, edit, crisis, resolution, type-over,

Lesson Description

- Show students how to enrich their writing by adding detail—characteristics, setting elements, pithier words, sensory input.
- This is a formative exercise, designed to hone writing strategies through active learning and authentic assessments.

Computer Activity

Note: If you don't have Word, use your school's word processing program.

- Add your name at top of an MS Word doc (font size 12, Times New Roman).
- Leave a double space for the title. Students will come up with that at the end of the story.
- Read a rudimentary story to the class, maybe one they wrote the prior year. Ask them why it sounds so amateurish. You'll probably get answers like detail, word selection, description.
- Have students consider what would it be like if they were the main character, standing in that dank warehouse, looking for a frightened, shivering lost dog?
- Introduce story with a hook to grab the reader, i.e., *He smelled lilacs, like his mother's perfume, but she'd been gone for five years.*
- Characterization: In the next paragraph, tell about the main character. How does s/he walk? What's s/he wearing? Does s/he appear nervous? Calm? Hurried? If you want to have two, tell me about the second through the eyes of the protagonist.
- Setting: In the next paragraph, tell me where s/he is. What do his/her senses notice—what does s/he see/smell? Is there a taste to the air from a factory or a volcano nearby? Can s/he smell freshly-mown grass, or hear cows lowing in the distance? What's that chugging noise to the left? Is it dangerous?
- Now, the plot. What problem does the main character face? How does it threaten her/him? Can you see the concern/worry in the way s/he walks, her/his posture, movements? Is s/he carrying

anything that would provide us with a clue?

- Spend the rest of the story reaching a crisis and then resolve it. It might only take a few paragraphs, or more. You decide.
- Final step: Proof read. Are there more interesting synonyms for any of the words chosen? Have any words been overused, like *boy* or *ran*? If so, close your eyes, think about the individual and describe him differently. *Skinny kid*, or *lanky-limbed youth*. If you say he's *running*, is he *galloping* like a horse, *jogging*, maybe *sprinting*? Watch him in your mind (he's your character) and paint a word picture of what he's really like.
- Check for spelling errors (red squiggly lines) and grammar errors (green squiggly lines). Make sure you remain in one tense throughout—present or past—and one person (usually first or third). Allow only five 'was' words. More makes the story too passive.
- In this story, there's nothing fancy about formatting. Pick Times New Roman or Ariel. No clipart, borders, or Word art.
- Print; save to student network folder; save-as to flash drive

Extensions

- Before beginning, give the students a plain story (such as the one below) and have them collaboratively enhance it with character, setting and plot details.

Troubleshooting Tips

- *I'm trying to edit, but I'm typing over each word instead of inserting. (Push the 'insert' key—to the right of the backspace)*

His fur was mangy and falling out in spots. And his bright white teeth had yellowed with the diet of grasses he ate. He had...

Its trunk was craggy and thick, and its arms spread wide over the grass as though welcoming Mr. Coyote.

"Mr. **Coyote** was getting very <u>old</u> and had to be more careful for his own safety. H had been <u>walking</u> for hours and hours through a <u>beautiful</u> valley when he came upon a large **tree**.

Mr. Coyote was very tired and wanted to <u>rest</u> but he also **needed to be safe**. He kindly asked the tree, "Please open up so I can rest safely in your e".

How had he gotten himself in such a fix? For a wily coyote, he'd sure been stupid the last few days. Surely, he could find a way out of this mess, but first, he had to rest his paws.

Subject #2: Composition and Communication

Project #34: What Does a Dolch Word Look Like? (in KidPix) Have students type three or four of their site/spelling words into KidPix. Create a quasi-sentence, filling in the missing nouns, verbs, etc., with stamps from KidPix toolbars.

Higher-order thinking skills	Technology-specific:	Subject Area/ Learning-specific	Standard: ISTE
Analyzing Applying	*Formatting text, multimedia communication, format pictures*	*Spelling, grammar, communication*	*1c, 6c*

Grade level: K-2
Prior knowledge: Project 1 and 2 (KidPix Basx I and II)
Time required: 30 minutes
Software required: KidPix (or your class art tool)
Vocabulary: Dolch, high-frequency, sight words, stamps, toolbar, multimedia, multiple intelligences,

Lesson Description

- This project covers two critical learning issues: 1) students learn in different ways, and 2) there's a list of words that appear over and over in what children hear and see. They're worth learning.
- Referred to as Multiple Intelligences, and popularized by Howard Gardner, Multiple Intelligences are seven different ways to teach children and adults. The ones we pay attention to in this lesson are text, color, and pictures.
- The most common words in the English language—called Dolch words, high-frequency words or sight words (because they aren't phonetic; you just have to recognize them)—account for an amazing amount of words in children's literature. According to the National Literacy Strategy; "these words play an important part in holding together the general coherence of texts..." According to Robert Hillerich, "Just three words *I, and, the* account for ten percent of all words in printed English."

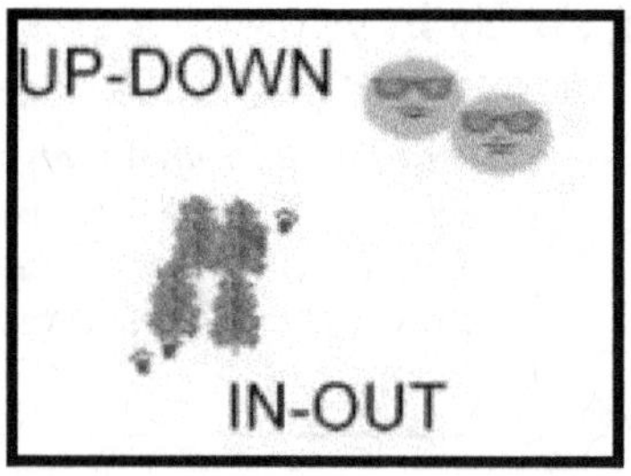

- In a nutshell: The main reason for knowing Dolch words is you will see them again and again.

Computer Activity

Note: If you don't have KidPix, use your school's digital drawing program.

- Collect grade-level Dolch/high-frequency words (see list below).
- Put several together in a sentence.
- Have students open KidPix. Use the ABC text tool to write these words. Use caps lock for younger with no emphasis on grammar. Have the older learners capitalize the first letter of the sentence and

add a period at the end. Discuss how this is good grammar.

- Have students add stamps, stickers or the spray can to enhance the sentence's meaning with pictures, colors, movement of their choice.

Extensions

- Instead of creating a sentence, use words that are opposites, i.e., up and down, in and out. Incorporate discovery into this lesson by asking students what they think goes up and down. What goes in and out? The two examples in this project, I got from students. Have them draw a picture of something going up and down (see inset).
- Choose words with similar beginning sounds, vowel sounds or endings.

Troubleshooting Tips

- *Students can't relate the words to events (Help them by discussing what goes up and down, in and out, over and under. Help them see the word as a symbolic representation of an action.)*

List of Dolch words

Pre-K	Kindergarten	First	Second	Third
a, and, away, big, blue, can, come, down, find, for, funny, go, help, here, I, in, is, it, jump, little, look, make, me, my, not, one, play, red, run, said, see, the, three, to, two, up, we, where, yellow, you	all, am, are, at, ate, be, black, brown, but, came, did, do, eat, four, get, good, have, he, into, like, must, new, no, now, on, our, out, please, pretty, ran, ride, saw, say, she, so, soon, that, there, they, this, too, under, want, was, well, went, what, white, who, will, with, yes	after, again, an, any, as, ask, by, could, every, fly, from, give, giving, had, has, her, him, his, how, just, know, let, live, may, of, old, once, open, over, put, round, some, stop, take, thank, them, then, think, walk, were, when	always, around, because, been, before, best, both, buy, call, cold, does, don't, fast, first, five, found, gave, goes, green, its, made, many, off, or, pull, read, right, sing, sit, sleep, tell, their, these, those, upon, us, use, very, wash, which, why, wish, work, would, write, your	about, better, bring, carry, clean, cut, done, draw, drink, eight, fall, far, full, got, grow, hold, hot, hurt, if, keep, kind, laugh, light, long, much, myself, never, only, own, pick, seven, shall, show, six, small, start, ten, today, together, try, warm

Sites for Dolch and High-Frequency Words

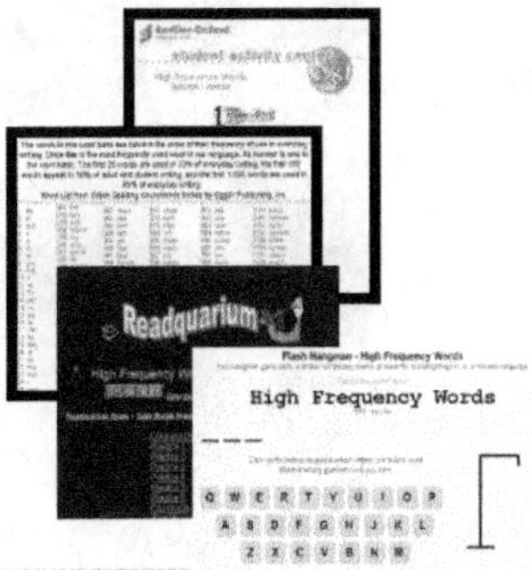

High-frequency words, with games to reinforce their use

High-frequency word games and activities:

High Frequency Words Hangman

Subject #2: Composition and Communication

Project #35: Sponge Activities for Vocabulary Building. There are lots of great online vocabulary websites to help kids learn high-frequency and Dolch words. I'll share five of them. that make vocabulary fun.

Higher-order thinking skills	Technology-specific:	Subject Area/ Learning-specific	Standard: ISTE
Applying—use concepts in new situations	*Use technology to broaden subject matter competency, learn the basics of internet*	*Reinforce spelling, class word lists*	*1d, 2b*

Grade level: K-4
Prior knowledge: Project 99 (Internet Basx) if you have Book II available
Time required: 5-10 minutes
Software required: Browser
Vocabulary: high-frequency, Dolch, links, favorites, bookmarks

Lesson Description

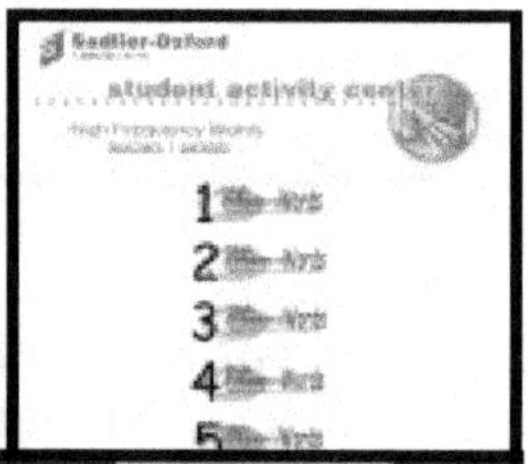

- The term "sponge" was originally coined by Madeline Hunter as an activity designed to produce learning during the time taken up by "administrivia." These sponges stem from the philosophy that there should be no wasted moments in her classroom.
- Each website offers quick activities that take 5-10 minutes before lunch, between activities, etc.
- Ctrl+click the blue links or images to go to the site

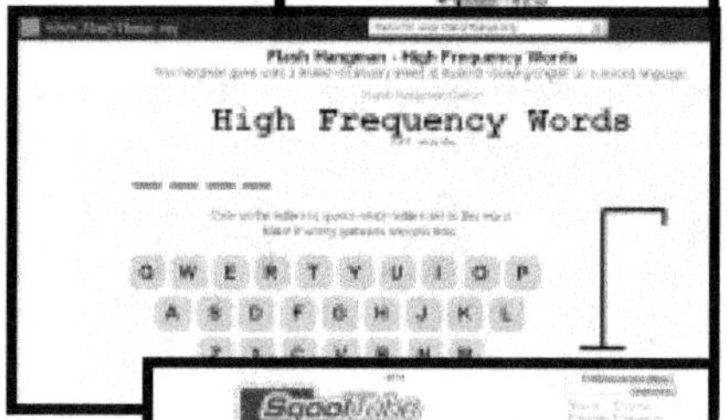

Computer Activity

- Play the popular game Hangman with high-frequency words
- SqoolTube videos on reading, comprehension, phonics, sign language (similar to YouTube, but school-friendly)
- Dolch Words Typing Test

Extensions

- Add the websites to favorites, your homescreen, or wherever you curate links for use in your classroom so that students can access them quickly

Troubleshooting Tips

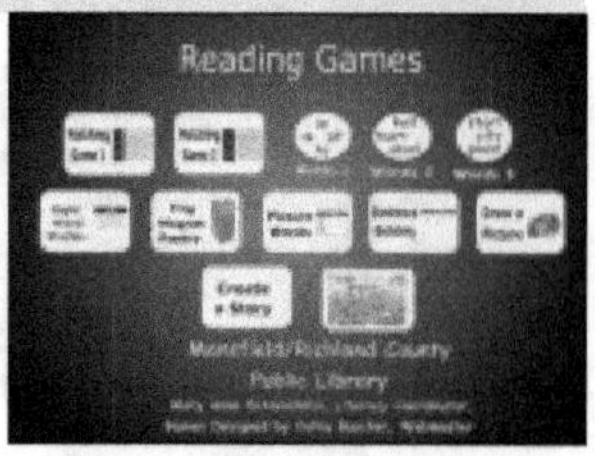

- *I get a list of hits—not the site (Did you type the address into your browser's search bar rather than the address bar?)*
- *The site doesn't come up (it may be a dead link. Links die—that's just how it is. Select a different site).*

Subject #2: Composition and Communication

Project #36: My First Report (in Word) Students type a report on one of the class units of inquiry (i.e., animals) using MS Word. Use this lesson to introduce MS Word, margins, page breaks, centering, fonts, etc. Show students how to add pictures from the internet and from the computer.

Higher-order thinking skills	Technology-specific:	Subject Area/ Learning-specific	Standard: ISTE
Analyzing, applying, evaluating	*Use of software effectively and productively*	*History, culture, language arts (reading and comprehension)*	*3a-d*

Grade level: 2-3
Prior knowledge: Computer Basx, Project 16 *A Holiday Memory* (Must use MS Word) or 17 *A Holiday Story*
Time required: 45 minutes, 4 sessions
Software required: KidPix, Word (or class word processing and art tools)
Vocabulary: paginate, footer, ctrl, Word, image, border, tab, indent, font, number sign, align-left

Lesson Description

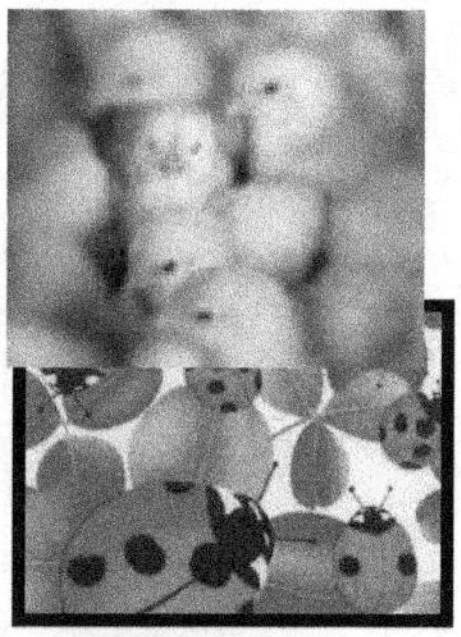

- Nothing teaches like a report. Nothing is more fun than pictures.
- Put both together for a second/third grade collaborative learning experience that activates their critical thinking and engages them in their own learning.
- This project can be done in conjunction with #88 *Elementary Research*

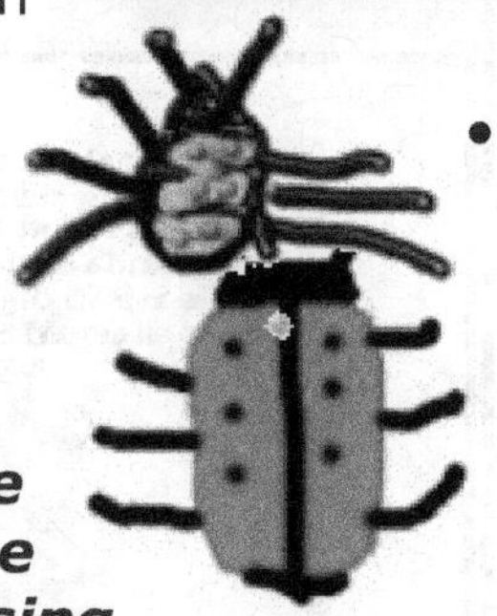

Computer Activity

Note: If you don't have KidPix or Word, use school word processing and drawing programs.

- Draw a picture of the animal they are writing about with the digital pencil or paint brush. When finished, export.
- Open Google. Click the 'images' Images tab. Have students search for pictures of their animal. Save at least five images (full size) to each student's network file folder.

- Open MS Word. Create a cover page (see sample on next page) with selected animal, student name, teacher, and the KidPix picture they exported. Text should be font size 36, **bold**, any font. Center everything vertically and horizontally. Ctrl+Enter to force a new page.
- You should now be on Page 2. Add footer to the report with student name and page number.
- Center the section title (if included). Left-align paragraph. Indent each paragraph. Add a picture of animal between sections (see samples).

Extensions

- Add a border to the cover. Choose a line border, to complement the professional nature of the report.

Troubleshooting Tips

- *My page numbers don't show in the footer. (Did you push # on the footer toolbar, or did you use Shift+3?)*

Samples of Report Pages:

For my report I chose the butterfly. A butterfly is an insect. The butterfly eats plants. The butterfly lives in warm and cold areas. You can see butterfly's day and night.

ge of butterfly is an egg. The egg is tiny. he egg doesn't move .The egg has a ring. The egg stays in this stage for a

age is a caterpillar. A caterpillar is small rpillar has legs. The caterpillar crawls.

YOUR BUG OR ANIMAL

Your First and Last Name
Your Teacher

(Ctrl+Enter for new page)

The second stage is the duckling. The duckling is 20 inches long. The duckling has black, white and brown. It has two legs and two wings. My animals swim and walk. It feels solf a furry. The duck protect the duckling by there eyes sight. It stays in this stage for a month.

The animal am researching is the chicken. My animal is a bird. The chicken eats insects, seeds, grass, table scraps, potatoes and bread. The chicken lives in a henhouse and a chicken coop. The temperature my animal lives in is 95 degrees Fahrenheit. Usually you find chickens all around the world in farms. My animal is most active during the day.

Phase 1 of the life cycle!
My animal begins as an egg. The egg is two inches long and is approximately two ounces. The egg is tan and brown. The outer covering of the egg is hard. It helps protect the animal by its hard, outer shell. The egg stays in this stage for a few months.

The second stage of the chicken is the chick. The chick has yellow feathers with an orange beak and fluffy feathers. The chick has two wings and two legs. Covering of the

Subject #3: Geography

Project #37: Oregon Trail. This simulation lets students experience a migration made by over 3,000 Americans as they traveled via wagon train to the wilds of the far west. Show students how to read headings on each screen, problem solve and apply simulation to classroom discussion on westward expansion. I include a worksheet of questions to answer as well as additional websites to extend their education

Higher-order thinking skills	Technology-specific:	Subject Area/ Learning-specific	Standard: ISTE
Analyzing, applying, evaluating	*Use of software effectively and productively*	*History, culture, language arts (reading and comprehension)*	*2b, 3a, 3d*

Grade level: 3-5
Prior knowledge: Computer Basx
Time required: 45 minutes, 2 sessions
Software required: Oregon Trail
Vocabulary: supplies, cholera, landmark, hardships, diseases, simulations

Lesson Description

- *Oregon Trail* is an game inspired by its real-life namesake and designed to teach the realities of life in a wagon train. Players assume the role of wagon train members, traveling from Independence, Missouri to the Willamette Valley.

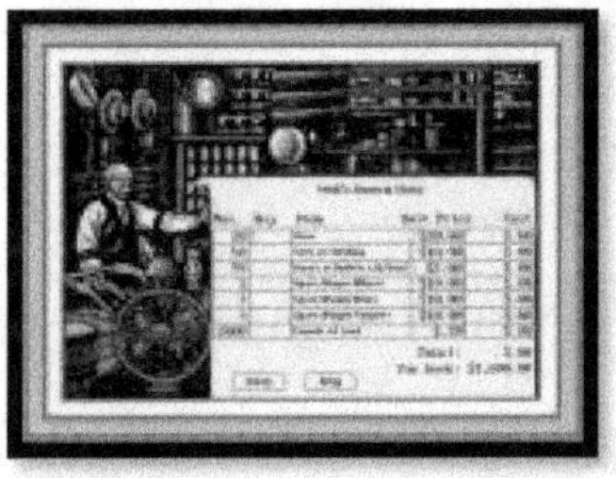

Computer Activity

- Open Oregon Trail. Have students start 'New Game' rather than 'Quick Start'. This force them to consider supplies needed vs. how much money they have and what will fit into a wagon. The game won't allow them to leave the initial town until a balance is achieved between these factors.

- As they travel, they fill out the guide sheet (see below). Most answers are found at the top of the screen where it explains what's happening.
- Pay attention to the screen bottom where it discusses the health, food supplies and morale of members.
- Because there weren't many towns along the Oregon Trail, students must find food by hunting, fishing, scavenging and/or trading with others.
- If a student can't find answers to questions, have them visit the suggested websites. The game takes only about 45 minutes, so they'll have plenty of time to research.
- If students must start their journey over, use 'Quick Start'.
- When finished, turn in.

Extensions

- Fill the questionnaire out on the computer. Toggle between the game and the sheet.

Troubleshooting Tips

- *The game froze (This happens occasionally no matter how well-managed a school lab. Start over with 'Quick Start'.)*
- *It keeps crashing (OT doesn't play well with Win7.)*

OREGON TRAIL—Beginners Edition

*Your Name:*____

*Your teacher:*____

As you play "Oregon Trail", fill in the answers to the questions:

1. Name two states the Oregon Trail crossed through.
   a. ____
   b. ____

2. Name two reasons settlers headed out on the Oregon Trail?
   a. ____
   b. ____

3. Describe a covered wagon

   ____

4. Describe five supplies you bought for the trip.
   a. ______________________ d. ______________________
   b. ______________________ e. ______________________
   c. ______________________

5. Describe two landmarks you encountered
   a. ____
   b. ____

6. List two hardships you faced
   a. ____
   b. ____

7. List two diseases your wagon train got.
   a. ____
   b. ____

8. List two types of weather you encountered.
   a. ____
   b. ____

9. List two mistakes made on the trail.
   a. ____
   b. ____

10. How did you solve problems on the trail?
   a. ____
   b. ____

OREGON TRAIL—Advanced Edition

*Your Name:*____________________

*Your teacher:*____________________

OREGON TRAIL

Fill this guide out as you play the game.

1. **List 3 reasons why settlers headed out on the Oregon Trail:**
   a. ____________________
   b. ____________________
   c. ____________________
2. **Describe a covered wagon and 3 supplies it carried:**

   ____

   ____

   a. ____________________
   b. ____________________
   c. ____________________
3. **Name 3 states the Oregon Trail crossed through:**
   a. ____________________
   b. ____________________
   c. ____________________
4. **List 3 hardships settlers faced:**
   a. ____________________
   b. ____________________
   c. ____________________
5. **List 3 diseases settlers faced:**
   a. ____________________
   b. ____________________
   c. ____________________
6. **List 3 types of weather settlers encountered and where it was (a state or a biome):**
   a. ________________
   b. ________________
   c. ________________
7. **List 3 landmarks settlers passed on the trail and where they were:**
   a. ________________
   b. ________________
   c. ________________
8. **What were 3 mistakes settlers made on the trail and how could they solve them:**
   a. ________________
   b. ________________
   c. ________________
9. **What are your conclusions about braving the Oregon Trail?**

   ____

   ____

How to Teach Problem-solving With Oregon Trail

My students love Oregon Trail. It fits nicely with a unit of inquiry in both 3rd and 4th grade. It makes important concepts easy because it puts them right at the top of the screen–*You die of malaria, You reach the Blue River.* I ask questions of students like *What were problems faced by settlers along the trail* (they caught diseases)? *What natural landmarks did they cross* (the Blue River)? I have 3rd graders fill out a questionnaire and I have 4th graders complete an expanded version digitally. They bring a Word doc up electronically and fill it out on the computer as they play the game.

This two-week unit is a big hit with students. Here's the problem. Oregon Trail doesn't play well with Win 7. It freezes, stalls, blows up. We've called the manufacturer, but no luck. At first, I was sorely disappointed to lose such a valuable simulation. All of the 'trail' series are wonderful–Amazon Trail, Inca Trail, Yukon Trail. The only one that is networked is Oregon Trail, so I limited myself to that one, not wanting the confusion of CD's popping in and out of drives and getting scratched and broken.

Then I had an epiphany as I watched students work through the stalls and freezes. They wanted to know how to fix the problems so they could continue with the game. Wow. What better way to teach problem solving than to teach it with real-life situations that students are motivated to solve? It's turned into a successful problem-solving lesson.

Here's what we learn:

- When the program freezes, they learn that **Alt+F4** will close programs most of the time so they can restart
- If Alt+F4 doesn't work, they learn how to get to the **Task Manager with Ctrl+Alt+Del.**
- They learn that once in the task manager, they go to **'applications', select the offending program and click 'end task'**. All of us have had to do that. Now the kids know how
- Sometimes, Oregon Trail is hidden behind a black screen. Students learn to use **Alt+Tab** to cycle through open screens
- Sometimes, the program collapses to the taskbar. Students learn to **check the taskbar** for open programs, click on the one they want and re-open

Problem solving is an important part of technology. Computers never go smoothly and progressing past these speed bumps is the most frustrating part of working with tech. Through this lesson, students learn that it's part of life, that problems can be solved, and they accept them without the drama of throwing the computer away and starting over.

I will probably continue with this program next year, with an introduction that they aren't just learning about settlers.

Subject #3: Geography

Project #38: Introduction to Google Earth Google Earth can be used for many classroom activities. It is a favorite of even my kindergartners. I start by showing them how to pan in and out, drag to move the globe, change the perspective of the earth's surface, use the built in tour or one I add. I have fifth graders create a tour that the youngers then watch.

Higher-order thinking skills	Technology-specific:	Subject Area/ Learning-specific	Standard: ISTE
Analyzing, evaluating	*Adding graphic to KidPix, saving image in Google Earth,*	*Critical thinking, research, information fluency*	*3a-d*

Grade level: K-4
Prior knowledge: None
Time required: 30 minutes
Software required: Google Earth (free download or use it directly from the web)
Vocabulary: demo, tour, greeting, bathymetry, 3D,

Lesson Description

- Google Earth is a virtual globe browser, drawing on thousands of satellite pictures to present our world. It is used by hundreds of millions of people, thousands of which contribute to its wiki tools for uploading data and info.
- Google Earth is a hugely popular program with students as young as kindergarten

Computer Activity

Note: If you don't have Google Earth, use your school's mapping program (i.e., Scribble Map).

- Take a tour of Google Earth. Discover the power of Google Earth. Allow time so students can stop and start, pan in and out, explore an interesting location.
- Next, show student how to use the 'fly to' field

to designate a location. Type in, say 'Eiffel Tower' and push enter. Watch how GE flies around the world and pans into the location. Type in their address and visit a bird's eye view of their house.

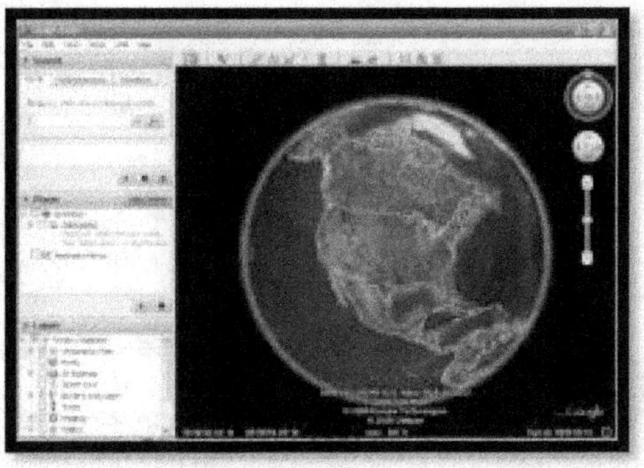

- Explain mouse tools for GE:
  - Use mouse scroll to pan in, out
  - Use left click to stop panning.
  - Click and drag the mouse scroll to change perspective.
  - Click and drag the globe to move location
- Give students a list culled from classroom lessons and wonders of the world—or their suggestions. Have plenty of helpers for the younger students. Allow time to find the prescribed locations and explore the area. Encourage students to investigate.

Extensions

- Show how to select '3D buildings' on the toolbar (under layers) and watch the buildings pop up into three dimensions.

- Try 'Street View' from the toolbar to see an eye-level view of the world (through the cameras)
- Try 'Sky' to tour outer space
- Try 'Google Ocean' to cruise the 3D bathymetry of our underwater world.
- Use 'flight simulator'—a free tool that allows students to fly around the world in an F16 or bi-plane. This is a favorite at my school.
- Add additional Google Earth skills for advanced learners (i.e., grids, measurements, marking locations)

Troubleshooting Tips

- *I type in a location and GE can't find it. (Add the city, state, country, or some combination of those. Or, go to 'Help—Google Earth Community' and find it there.)*

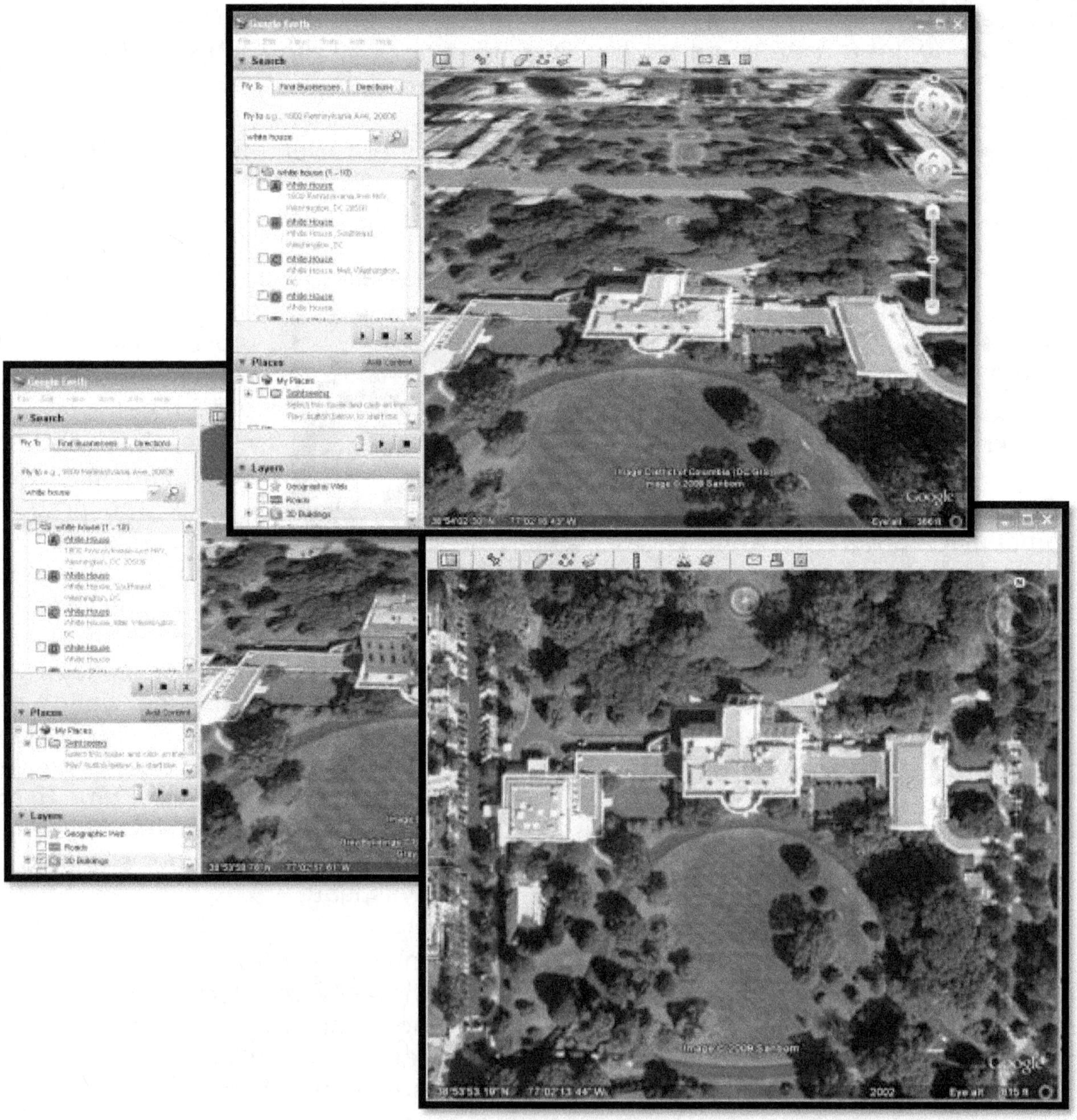

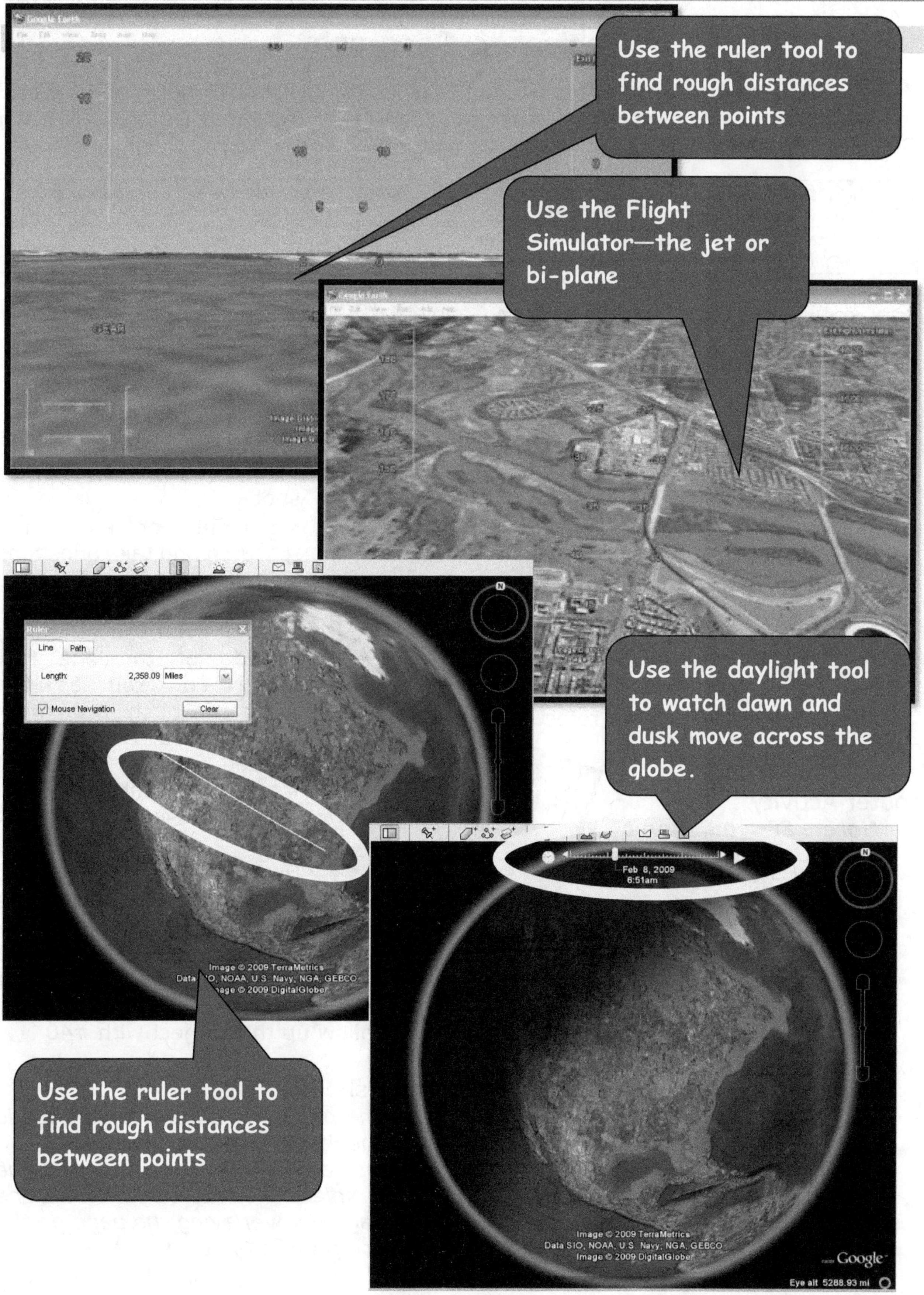
Use the ruler tool to find rough distances between points
Use the Flight Simulator—the jet or bi-plane
Ruler
Line
Path
Length: 2,358.09 Miles
Mouse Navigation
Clear
Use the daylight tool to watch dawn and dusk move across the globe.
Feb 8, 2009
6:51am
Use the ruler tool to find rough distances between points
Image © 2009 TerraMetrics
Data SIO, NOAA, U.S. Navy, NGA, GEBCO
Image © 2009 DigitalGlobe
Google
Eye alt 5288.93 mi

Subject #3: Geography

Project #39: Google Earth Board. Students select from a list of Wonders of the World (or locations that support a classroom unit). Students research it, locate it using Google Earth and make a short presentation to the class.

Higher-order thinking skills	Technology-specific:	Subject Area/ Learning-specific	Standard: ISTE
Analyze, apply, understand	*Graphics formatting, Google Earth basics*	*Presentation skills, research and information fluency*	*3a-d*

Grade level: 3-7
Prior knowledge: Project 38 (Intro to Google Earth)
Time required: 45 minutes to research, 10 minutes to present
Software required: Google Earth, browser
Vocabulary: Wonders of the World, fly to, doc, download, ruler, image, overlay

Lesson Description

- Student researches a geographic location or one discussed in class, and shares one amazing fact about it.
- Preparation is only 45 minutes--so students focus research on one fact that grabs their attention (see list under Project 40).

Computer Activity

Note: If you don't have Google Earth, do this project without that element.

- Students select a location and a date for their presentation.
- Students research their location, evaluating which of the many facts would be the most interesting to their classmates. Encourage students not to stop at the first fact they find but select among several. Write the fact on the guide sheet
- Students find their location on Google Earth, refine it to an appealing view (perspective, distance, 3D view, etc.), resize it to fit spot on the guide sheet, print and paste it into that spot
- Student present their research and take questions from the audience. They are encouraged to attempt to answer even the questions outside of the one fact researched. You as the teacher can pitch in answers when possible. I was always amazed at the depth of interest students had once their curiosity was peaked.

Extensions

- Place the Wonders of the World on the Google Earth globe
- Have student find the distance from their Wonder of the World to their house using Google's ruler
- Follow up this project with #40

Troubleshooting Tips

- *The picture is too big for the guide sheet. (Save the image and insert it into a Word doc. Resize using the handles. Check to be sure it fits the page by overlaying the page on the computer monitor. Print)*

GOOGLE EARTH BOARD SIGN-UP

Pick a date and a location—so sign your name twice

Signups can also be completed via a Google Form or SignUp Genius

	Class A	B	C
Week of *			
Week of *			
Week of *			
Week of *			
Week of *			
Week of *			
Week of *			
Week of *			
Week of *			

GOOGLE EARTH BOARD TOPICS

	Class #1	Class #2	Class #3	Class #4
Ayers Rock				
Death Valley				
Egyptian Pyramids				
Great African Rift				
Great Barrier Reef				
Great Wall of China				
Hagia Sophia, Istanbul				
Hoover Dam				
Istanbul				
Leaning Tower of Pisa				
Mt. Everest				
Mt. St. Helens				
Ngorongoro Crater				
Panama Canal				
San Andreas Fault				
Stonehenge				
Straits of Gibraltar				
Suez Canal				
Taj Mahal				
The Chunnel				
The Eiffel Tower				
The Red Sea				
The Ross Ice Shelf				
Tierra del Fuego				
Vatican City				
Victoria Falls				

GOOGLE EARTH BOARD GRADING

Name: ______________________________

Class: ______________________________

You shared an interested fact with the class ____________

You spoke loudly enough for all to hear ____________

You seemed knowledgeable ____________

You had a calm, confident presence ____________

You didn't use vocal cues that showed nervousness ____________

You didn't use visual cues that showed nervousness ____________

You looked your audience in the eye as you talked ____________

Overall impression ____________

Subject #3: Geography

Project #40: The Wonders of Google Earth. Students create their own tour on Google Earth using locations selected by the classroom teacher or of interest to themselves. They add the locations to Google Earth, add a fact about it and turn it into a tour

Higher-order thinking skills	Technology-specific: Google Earth	Subject Area/ Learning-specific	Standard: ISTE
Analyze, apply, understand	*Select/use applications effectively and productively*	*Presentation skills, research and information fluency*	*3a-d*

Grade level: 5-8
Prior knowledge: Project 38 (Intro to Google Earth), Project 39 (Google Earth Board)
Time required: 45 minutes, 3 sessions
Software required: Google Earth (free download or web-based)
Vocabulary: fly-to, pin, toolbar, tour, 'my places', right click, temporary places

Lesson Description

- Create an automated tour of the same locations researched and presented for the Google Earth Board (Project 39)

Computer Activity

Note: If you don't have Google Earth, use Scribble Map, Bing Maps, or another mapping alternative.

- Pass out a list you've developed of all facts collected from the Google Earth Board presentations or get these from classroom teacher for locations they've visited during class. Zoom in on the figure below for ideas:

WONDERS OF GOOGLE EARTH TOUR FACTS

Collected from student reports—you'll collect your own list

LOCATION	IN TERESTING FACTS
Ayers Rock	❖ One of the oldest rocks on Earth. ❖ Perimeter is 5 miles ❖ Has a waterfall called Alice Springs ❖ Changes colors depending upon the time of day
Death Valley	❖ Record for highest temperature in the Western hemisphere—134 degrees ❖ Second hottest recorded temperature in the world ❖ Lowest spot in North America at 282 feet below sea level
Egyptian Pyramids	❖ Pyramids are so large they can be seen from the Moon ❖ The oldest structures in existence ❖ They are oriented north-south ❖ There are around 110 Egyptian pyramids
Eiffel Tower	❖ Building started in 1887; completed in 1889 for the World Fair ❖ 324 meters tall, made out of 9441 tons of wrought iron ❖ Repainted every 7 years; requires 50 tons of brown paint in 3 different shades ❖ More than 200,000 people visited it during the World's Fair of 1889
Great African Rift	❖ Named by a 19th century British explorer named John Walter Gregory ❖ 3700 miles long, extending from Jordan to South Africa ❖ Site of the oldest human remains (3.7 million year old Lucy)
Great Wall of China	❖ Isn't a continuous wall. ❖ Stretches 4,000 miles ❖ Guarded by 2-3 million soldiers ❖ Built 2,000 years ago by first emperor of China; rebuilt many times
Hagia Sophia	❖ 'Hagia Sophia' means *the church of the old wisdom* in Greek ❖ One of several great churches built by Constantine the Great in the 4th Century ❖ Started as a patriarchal basilica, became a mosque and is now a museum
Istanbul	❖ First known as Byzantium and then Constantinople ❖ Third largest city in the world ❖ Use to be the capital of the East Roman Empire and the Ottoman Empire ❖ Located in Turkey, whose main religion is Islam
Leaning Tower of Pisa	❖ Took 177 years to build; started 1173 ❖ 55.86 m tall on one side and 56.7 m tall on the other; weighs about 14,500 tons ❖ Took 70 tons of dirt to stabilize the tower in 2008 ❖ It has 294 steps
Madagascar	❖ Island created when it separated from India 80-100 million years ago ❖ 4th largest island in the world ❖ Despite proximity to Africa, no lions, giraffes, zebras, hippos here ❖ Home to 5% of the world's plants and animals
Mt. Everest	❖ Started growing about 60 million years ago ❖ 4000 people have attempted to climb it, but only 660 have succeeded. ❖ 142 people died attempting to climb Mt. Everest ❖ Rises a few millimeters each year due to geologic forces
Mt. St. Helens	❖ An active volcano in the Cascade range in the state of Washington ❖ It is young for a volcano, only about 40,000 years old ❖ Last erupted May 18, 1980, 8:32 am. ❖ Killed 57 people, destroyed 250 homes, 47 bridges, 185 miles of highway
Ngorongoro	❖ Haven for thousands of East African lions, elephants, wildebeests ❖ The crater of an extinct volcano ❖ The area around the crater was occupied by early man 3 million years ago

- Play the Google Earth sample tour that comes with the download called 'Sightseeing'. Notice how GE automatically zooms in on a location and then advances to the next.

- If there is a tour created by last year's students, have current students watch it. Point out locations, image display, tour order.
- Create a file folder called 'My Tour' under 'My Places'. Here, students will collect 5-10 locations for their tour.
- Use 'Fly To' field to find a location.
- Click 'Pin'  tool on toolbar; add site. In dialogue box, add one to three amazing facts from list you passed out. Here's an example below; you can see a larger image on the next page:

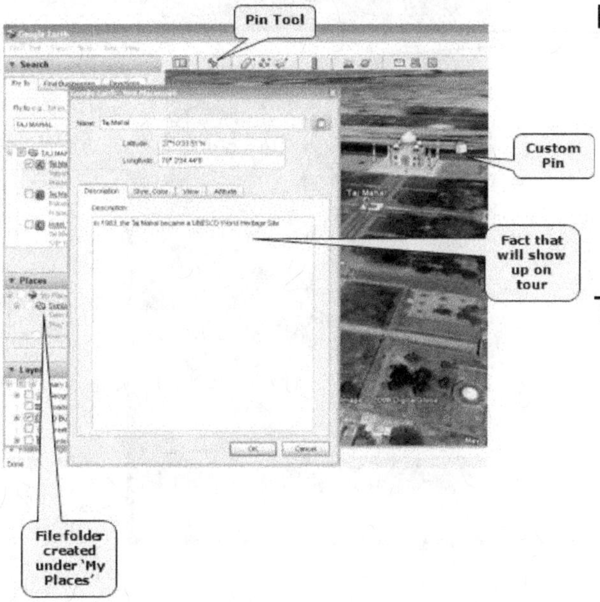

- Before closing, personalize pin. This can be by using one provided by Google Earth or uploading an image that identifies you—even your own face! Use the same look for all locations.

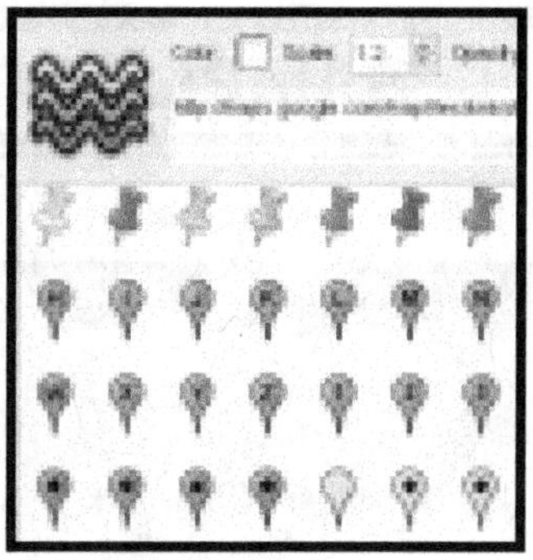

- Use Google Earth Community if you can't 'fly to' a location.
- Back up folder to flash drive
- When finished tour, press 'Play Tour'.

Extensions

- Use these tours to support geography units, history research, language arts, a book report or other
- Add a picture of the location using Add-Photo or Add-Image Overlay

Troubleshooting Tips

- *I can't get location to appear in my tour folder (Right click it wherever it shows up—probably 'Temporary Places'. Copy/ paste into your tour).*

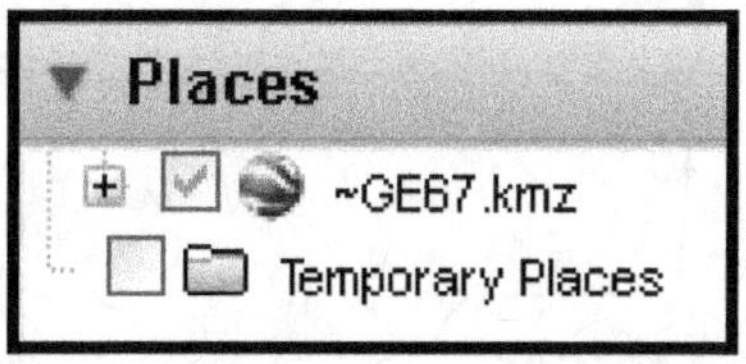

- *I can't find 'Temporary Places' (Be sure the 'Places' layer is expanded)*
- *My building isn't 3D (Check '3D Buildings' under 'Layers'?)*

SAMPLE TOUR 'PIN' IN GOOGLE EARTH

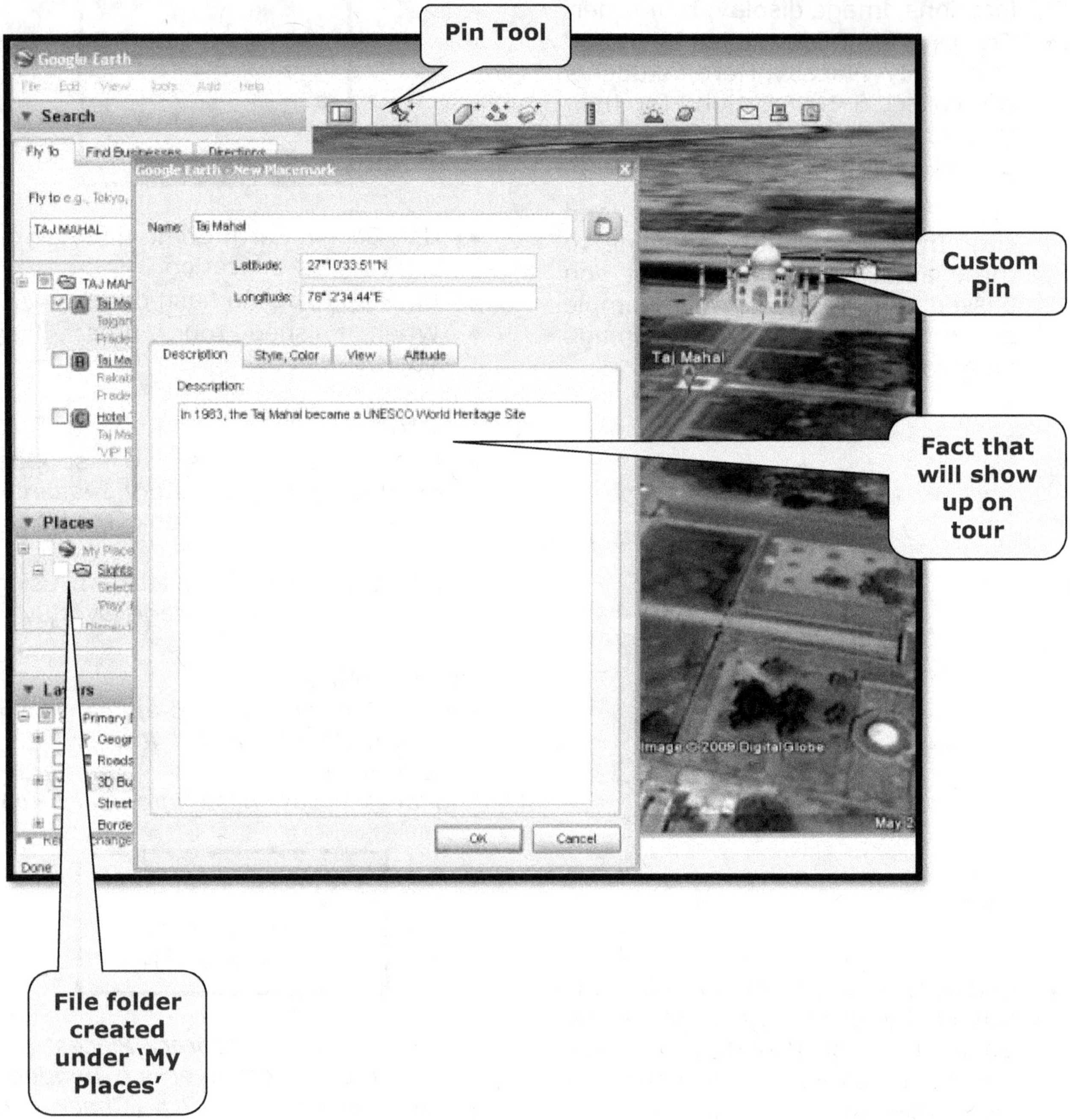

Subject #3: Geography

Project #41: Where is that? (Google Earth) Locate the Earth's major latitudes and longitudes using Google Earth. Locate cities, countries along the same latitude/longitude. Zoom in to see how exacting lats and longs get.

Higher-order thinking skills	Technology-specific:	Subject Area/ Learning-specific	Standard: ISTE
See patterns, organize parts, interpret facts	*Transfer current knowledge to new to broaden understanding*	*Lats and longs, explore the world*	*3a-d*

Grade level: 4-7
Prior knowledge: Google Earth tour/demo
Time required: 45 minutes
Software required: Google Earth (free download or web-based)
Vocabulary: lats and longs, pan, degrees-seconds-minutes, populate

Lesson Description

- Explore countries located on major latitudes and discuss what that means to climate, geology, etc.

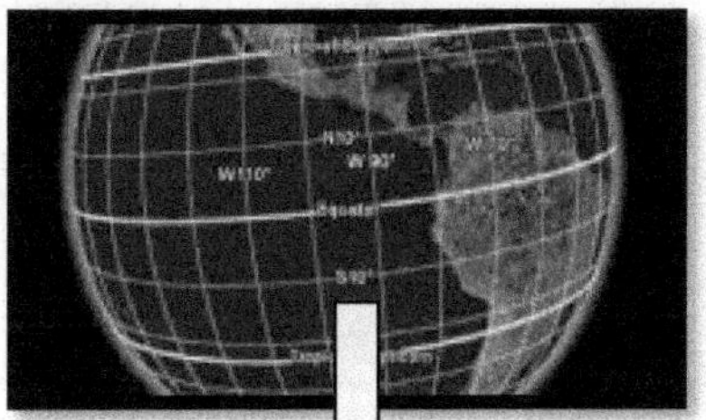

Computer Activity

Note: If you don't have Google Earth, use Scribble Map or another mapping alternative.

- Open Google Earth. Bring up latitude (lat) and longitude (long) lines by going to View-grid or Ctrl+L. Notice major lats and longs are yellow, others gray. Zoom in--notice how they populate as you pan in on a location.
- Discuss how lats and longs find a spot on earth. Explain minutes, seconds and degrees. Discuss uses of lats and longs.
- Explain what this means in terms of climate, biomes, habitats. For example, a country located along the equator will be hot year round. A country north of the arctic circle will be cold year round. Show students how to find countries located along each major latitude by clicking-dragging the globe along the major lat and see which countries can be found that cross it.
- Have students work in teams to complete worksheet on next page.
- If they are studying a spot in the world in class, have them locate it and determine its lat and long.

Extensions

- Have students find the latitude and longitude for their home
- Find the distance between their home and locations around the world using Google Earth's ruler.

Troubleshooting Tips

- *There is no International Date Line (it's called the Antemeridian on some versions of Google Earth—it's the back side of the Prime Meridian).*
- *I can't see which country the latitudes cross (turn on the 'Borders and Labels' layer. Zoom in or out to focus on the names.)*

Name: ____

Teacher: ____

Latitude and Longitude Practice

Find **two countries** that each major lat and long (latitude and longitude) listed below bisect:

1. Equator ____________________, ____________________
2. Tropic of Cancer____________________, ____________________
3. Arctic Circle____________________, ____________________
4. Tropic of Capricorn____________________, ____________________
5. Antarctic Circle____________________, ____________________
6. Prime meridian____________________, ____________________
7. International date line____________________, ____________________

My house is at ____________latitude and ______________longitude

What country is at N20, E80? ______________________________

What country is S85, E10? ______________________________

Subject #3: Geography

Project #42: Where Did I Come From? (KidPix, Google Earth) Students find their country of origin on Google Earth, grab a screen shot, save to their computer, import it into KidPix and add the country flag. Students learn about transferring data from one program to another as they proudly display their country of origin

Higher-order thinking skills	Technology-specific:	Subject Area/ Learning-specific	Standard: ISTE
Analyze, find patterns, Interpret facts	*Transfer knowledge to new technologies, broaden understanding in other areas*	*Lats and longs, explore the world*	*3a, 4b*

Grade level: 1-3
Prior knowledge: Project 1/2: KidPix Basx I/II, Project 38: Intro to GE, mouse basics
Time required: 45 minutes, might require 2 sessions
Software required: KidPix (or class art tool), Google Earth (free download or on web)
Vocabulary: virtual, satellite, graphic, drill down, toolbar, handles, drag-drop

Lesson Description

- Google Earth is used by millions of people as young as kindergarten, thousands of which contribute via its wiki tools by uploading data and buildings (via Google Sketch-up).
- Students use Google Earth to find their country of origin, copy it into KidPix, add the flag and their family name.

Computer Activity

Note: If you don't have KidPix or Google Earth, use the class version of the drawing program and mapping tool.

- Open Google Earth. Have student locate their country of origin via 'fly to' 

.
- Use the mouse scroll to zoom in or out until student has a perfect view of their country. Save image into student's network folder.
- Open KidPix. Add-add graphic, and drill down to the picture just saved from Google Earth. Double-click to add it. Use handles to adjust size.
- Go to stickers-flags, and have student find their country flag. Notice that the flag's country name is displayed at the bottom of the tool bar.
- Drag and drop flag into position. Resize with handles as needed.
- Select ABC text tool, font size 48, any font, any color.
- Type family name.
- Export picture to student folder and print with minimal assistance.

Extensions

- Have students add an interesting detail about their heritage to drawing
- Have students who are natives of other countries share their picture.

Troubleshooting Tips

- *It's not finding my country (are you in 'Directions' instead of 'fly to'?)*
- *I can't find my finished map (Did you* ***export*** *image as a .jpg or* ***save as*** *a .kpx? Few programs recognize the KidPix extension.)*
- *I can't resize my map (once you click out of the picture, you can no longer resize. Start over and resize before clicking out)*
- *This is too much! (Break the project into two lessons—just save the KidPix project in student file folder.)*

Subject #3: Geography

Project #43: Color My World (with KidPix). Import a globe template into KidPix. Students use the paint bucket to fill continents and oceans different colors, then label them as detailed as is age appropriate.

Higher-order thinking skills	Technology-specific:	Subject Area/ Learning-specific	Standard: ISTE
Apply information already learned	*Use of templates, adding text, formatting a document*	*Geography, colors, keyboarding, spelling, following directions*	*1d, 6c*

Grade level: 2-4
Prior knowledge: Project 1 and 2 (KidPix Basx I and II)
Time required: 30 minutes, might take 2 sessions
Software required: KidPix (or your class art tool)
Vocabulary: template, text, text tool, graphic, stickers, rubric, flash drive

Lesson Description

- With KidPix, students learn mouse skills, tools and toolbars, editing, text, and more. Thousands of projects have been designed with KidPix as their software.

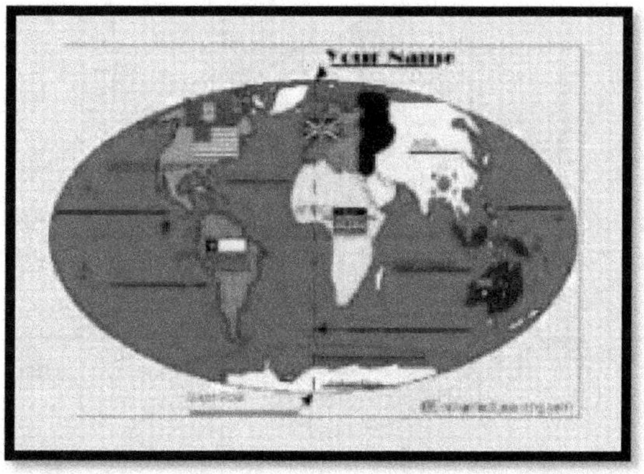

Computer Activity

Note: No KidPix? Use a class drawing program.

- Open KidPix. Have students Add graphic by drilling down to file folder with KidPix templates. This one requires the world with no words or colors. The example here is from Enchanted Learning.

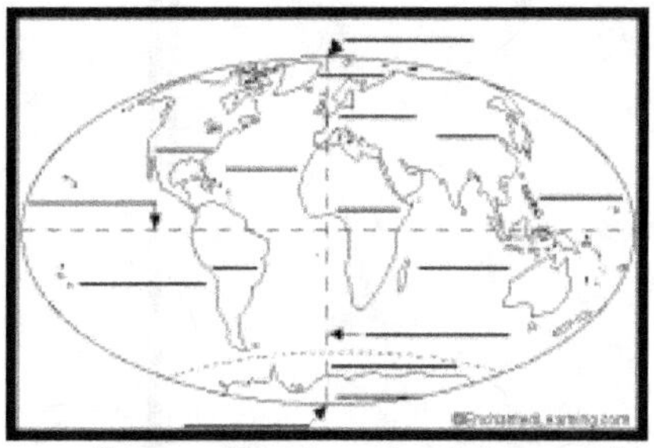

- Use ABC text tool, any font, size 10, any color, to label continents, oceans, even the equator.
- Use paint bucket  to fill continents and oceans, per directions (see following pages)
- Add national flags with stickers. Make country of origin the largest.
- Have students check rubric on the next pages to be sure all directions are done.
- Print without help; save to student folder; save-as to flash drive

Extensions

- Have students label oceans, lats and longs, and other geographic demarcations discussed in class.
- Go to Enchanted Learning for other templates that can be completed in KidPix or another drawing program.

Troubleshooting Tips

- *I poured blue into the ocean and it filled one of the continents. (That means the line around the continent wasn't completed. Click the Oops guy, redraw the black line around the continent and try again.)*

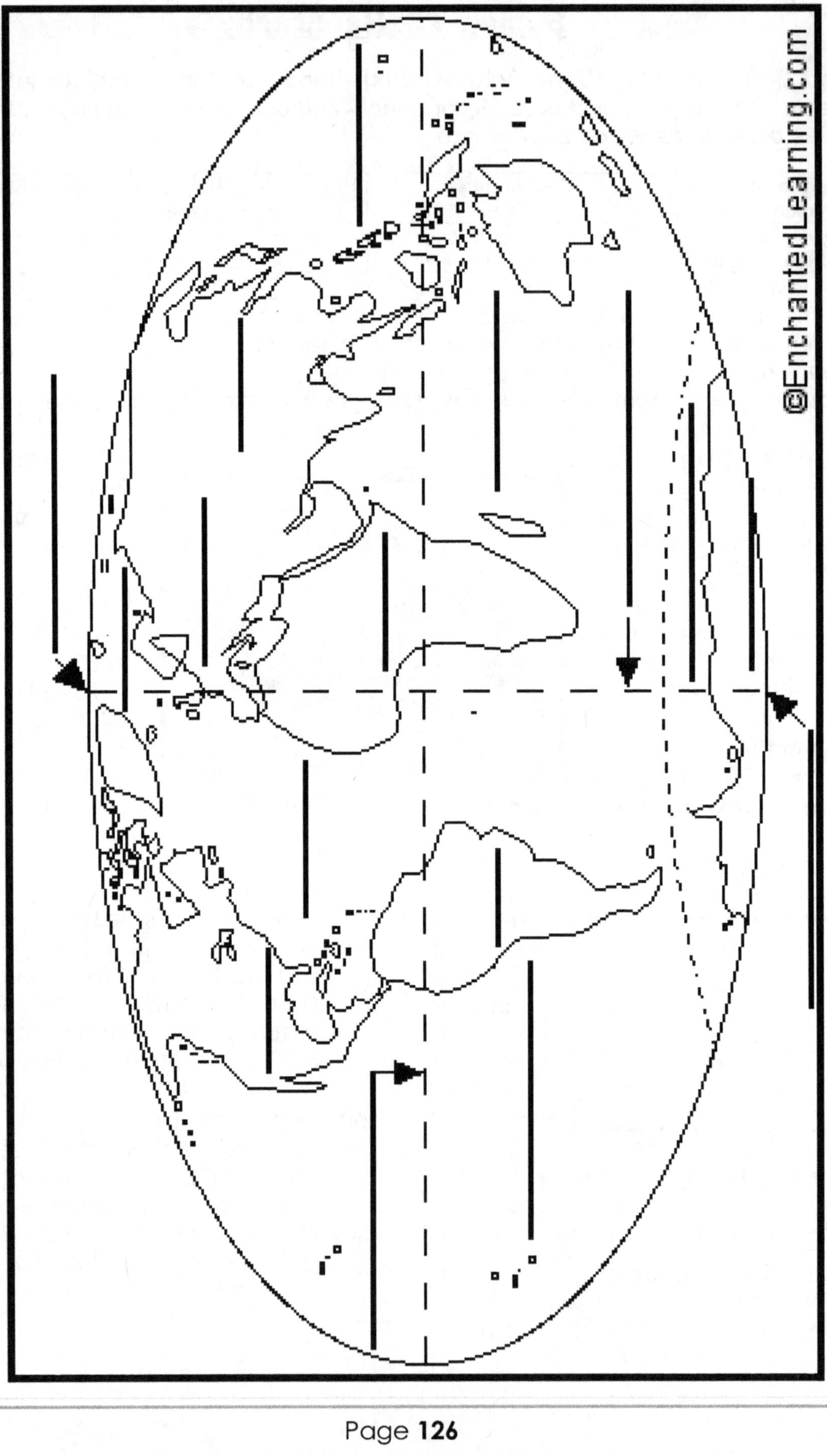
©EnchantedLearning.com

CONTINENT PROJECT

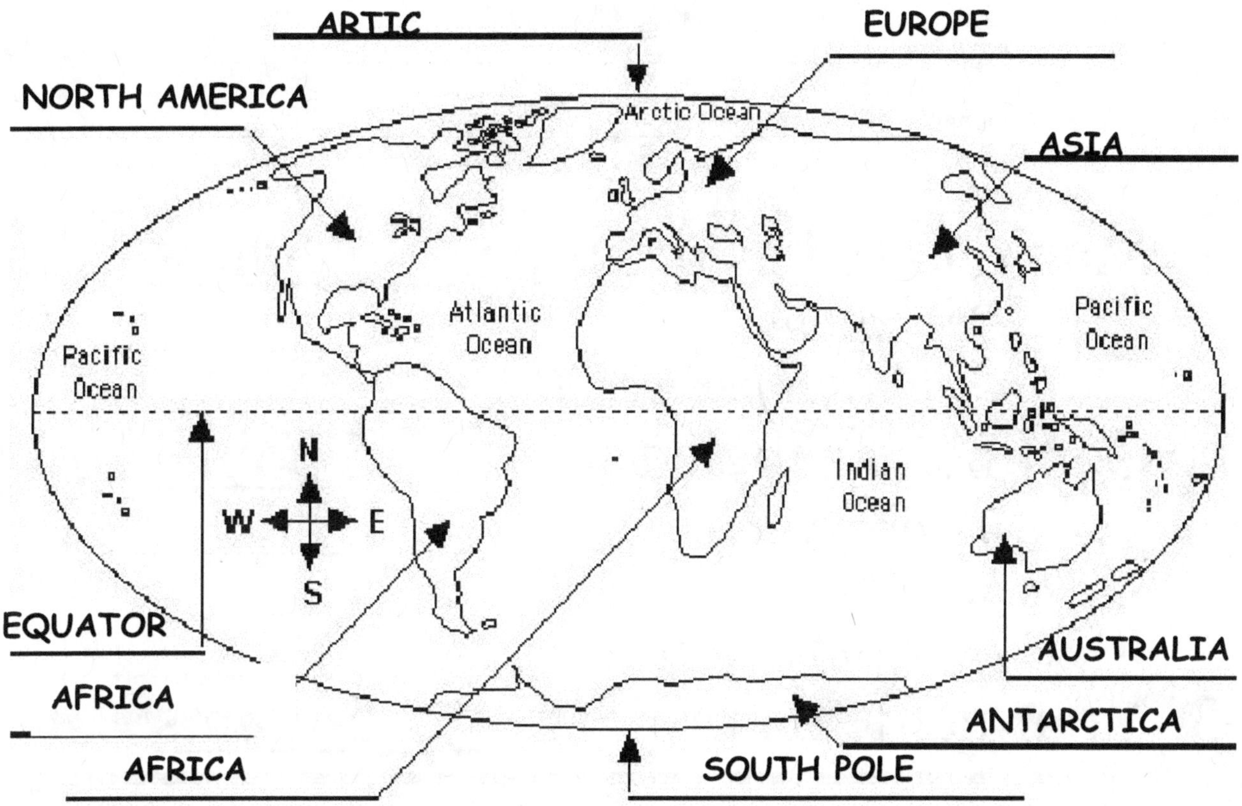

- Color Africa green
- Color Antarctica white
- Color Asia yellow
- Color Europe red
- Color Australia brown
- Color North America orange
- Color South America pink
- Color the oceans blue

Map Project
Grading Rubric

*Your name:*______________________________

*Teacher:*______________________________

1. Map colored as required ____5 points
    - *a. Oceans blue* ____________
    - *b. Continents per legend* ____________
2. Continents labeled ____5 points
    - *a. In correct spot* ____________
    - *b. Readable* ____________
    - *c. Fonts/sizes correct* ____________
3. Your name on project ____5 points

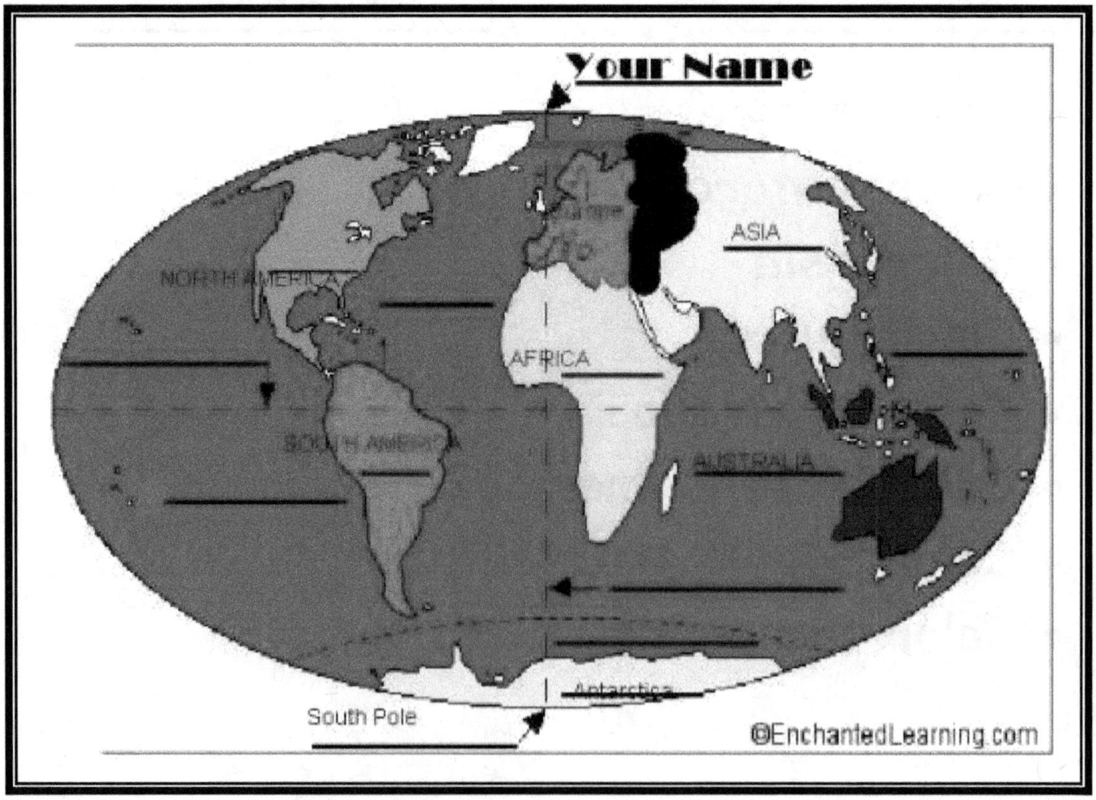

Subject #3: Geography

Project #44: What's 'NWSE'? (KidPix). Use a favorite program to teach directions, maps and compass roses. Create a cross. Label the four directions. Place a picture that coordinates with that direction by it.

Higher-order thinking skills	Technology-specific:	Subject Area/ Learning-specific	Standard: ISTE
Applying information, integrating knowledge	*Drawing tools, multimedia*	*Directions on a compass, Following directions*	*3d, 6b*

Grade level: 2-3
Prior knowledge: Project 1 and 2 (KidPix Basx I and II)
Time required: 30 minutes
Software required: KidPix (or your class art tool)
Vocabulary: compass, compass rose, directions, intersect, horizontal, vertical,

Lesson Description

- This project uses KidPix to create a compass. Directions can be marked by examples of a topic they are discussing, i.e., food, animals, etc., or the letters (see inset).

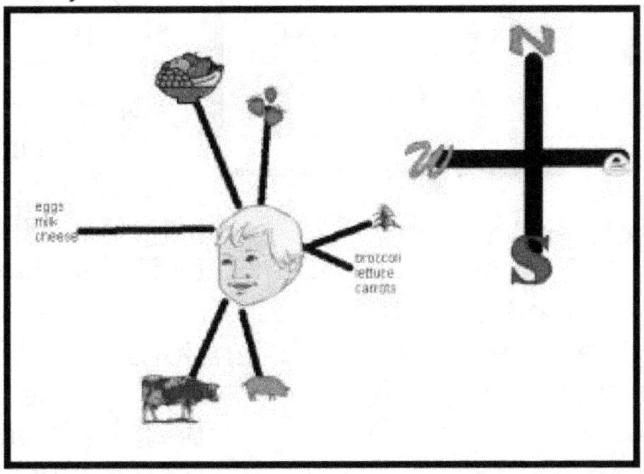

Computer Activity

Note: If you don't have KidPix, use another drawing tool.

- Students draw a cross with the pencil tool. Add directions.
- Discuss 'compass rose' as a class. Where do the letters come from? What does it mean by north, south, east, west—of what?
- Now place a picture in the canvas' middle (the student, a pet, etc.), in this case, the boy.
- Place a sticker from the focus topic at all four directions (i.e., fruit, farm animals, etc.) Discuss what students just did—placed a picture at the four main compass directions (see inset).
- Explain what the halfway point between the directions is—northeast, southwest, etc.
- Direct students to place a vegetable (or whatever the topic is) to the northwest of the central picture, a fruit (or ...) to the northeast, and so on.
- Print without help; save to student folder; save-as to flash drive

Extensions

- Do this project in pairs, allowing students to discuss what picture fits the requirements.
- Do a 'compass walk' around the school to discover what at school is at each of the directions. Write them down for students and add to drawing.

Troubleshooting Tips

- *I can't remember what those directions are (refer to the compass you marked with 'N', 'S', 'W' and 'E'.*
- *My line doesn't work (be sure you're on the straight line, not the curved one.*

Subject #3: Geography

Project #45: Where am I (using MS Word)? Use MS Word SmartArt to organize the Universe. Start with the student's town in the center and build out. Show students how to color the diagram. For olders, add a table at the bottom with the location and a fact about it. This is a great way to show kids how they can organize their thoughts with pictures, diagrams, tables—lots of ways other than simple text. Sometimes a picture is worth a thousand words.

Higher-order thinking skills	Technology-specific:	Subject Area/ Learning-specific	Standard: ISTE
Applying knowledge, creating, organizing,	*Insert graphics, organizers, format document*	*Geography, spelling*	*3b, 3c*

Grade level: 2-5
Prior knowledge: Introduction to MS Word
Time required: 30 minutes, 2 sessions (if completing extension table)
Software required: MS Word (or your class word processing tool)
Vocabulary: font, font size, sets, subsets, graphic organizer, diagram, menu

Lesson Description

- Use MS Word's graphic organizers to create a visual representation of where a student lives

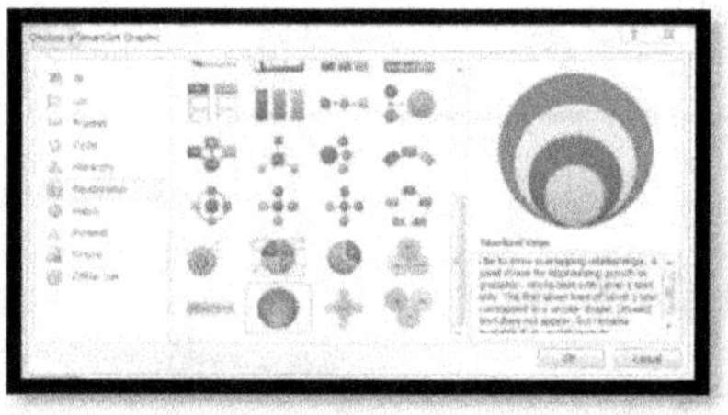

- This is an intro to sets and subsets. A group (set) is a subset of each target layer surrounding it. Therefore, the further inside the target, the more groups (sets) it is part of.

Computer Activity

Note: If you don't have Word, use another word processor.

- Put a heading at page's top (name, teacher, date, on separate lines).
- Center the title, *Where Am I*, font size 24, bold, underlined.
- Insert a SmartArt diagram from 'Relationship' category (a Venn diagram).
- The center of the target is the city where student lives. Build categories out with county, state, etc. The target only starts with three layers, so add six more.
  - Select 'change colors' on ribbon and format to taste.
  - Drag circles until they are evenly nested within the outer circle. Be sure not to hide text.
- Check spelling before printing. Save to folder; save-as to flash drive

Extensions

- Add a table underneath the graphic organizer with the same information (see Project 46: Landforms Table)

Troubleshooting Tips

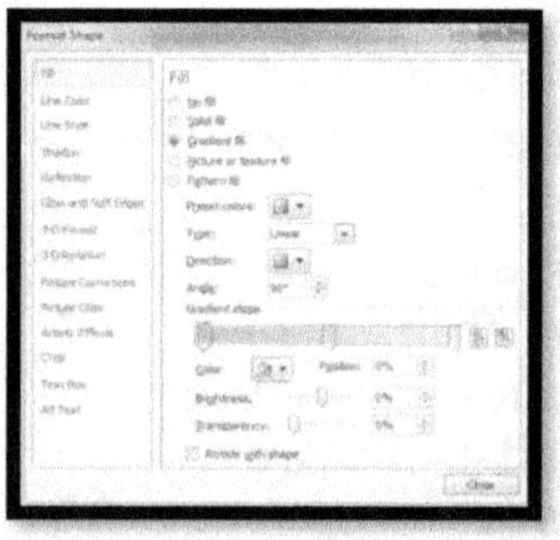

- *I can't find the diagram toolbar (Select 'SmartArt Tools at top of screen; right click on diagram, select 'format shape'.)*
- *The text won't fit in the space allowed in the diagram (Make font smaller or abbreviate.)*

WHERE AM I?

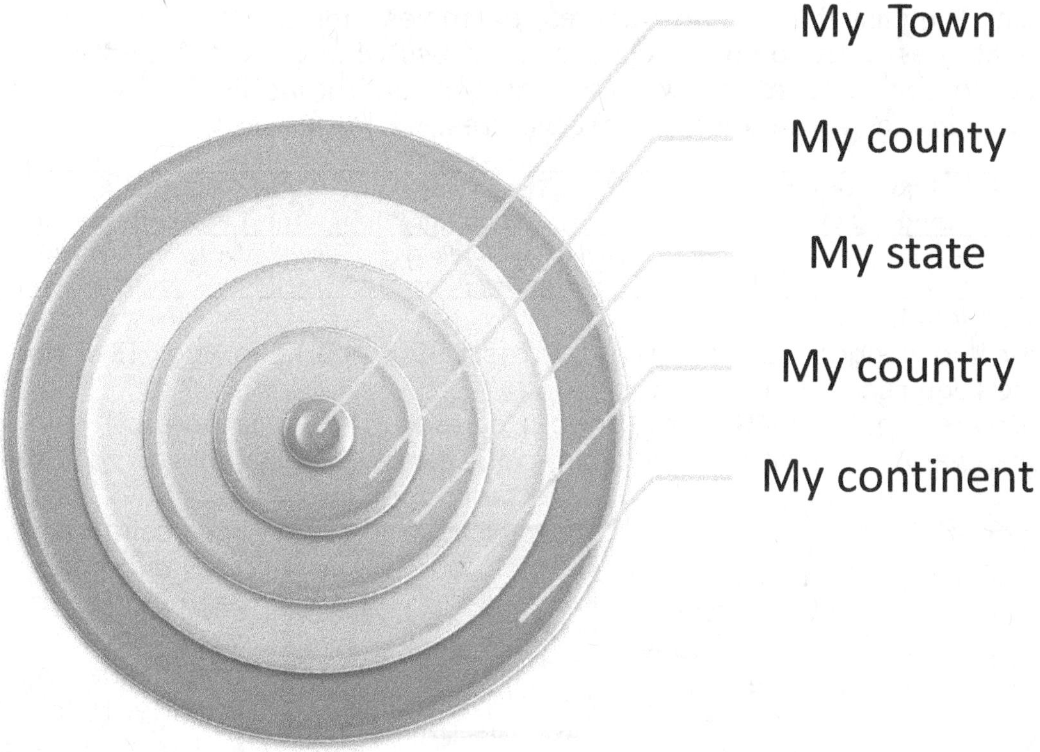

My city	
My county	
My state	
My country	
My continent	
My hemisphere	
My planet	*Earth*
My solar system	*The Solar System*
My galaxy	*The Milky Way*

Subject #3: Geography

Project #46: Landforms Table in Word. In this geography lesson, students use Microsoft Word to organize what they've learned about landforms into a three-column table. They list the landform names, examples, and attach a picture of each. Review the sites as a group so the class can discuss what makes a landform, etc. This is a great lesson to coordinate with a classroom unit of inquiry as well as teach students how to make Word tables, import pictures.

Higher-order thinking skills	Technology-specific:	Subject Area/ Learning-specific	Standard: ISTE
Analyze parts, identify components, organize	*Using tables: formatting/editing Adding pictures*	*Geography, science, spelling*	*3a-d, 6a, 6d*

Grade level: 3-5
Prior knowledge: Intro to Word, Project 99 if you have Book II of this collection
Time required: 45 minutes
Software required: MS Word (or your class word processing tool)
Vocabulary: landform, table, cell, search engine, tab, row, column, copy-paste

Lesson Description

Landform	Example	Picture
Desert	Sahara Desert Gobi Desert	
Rivers	Nile River Amazon Mississippi	
Lake	Lake Michigan Lake Victoria	

- Aligning text can be intimidating if you try to do it with tabs. Fortunately, the table feature does it effortlessly.
- In a table, columns and rows of text can easily be aligned, data added/deleted, theme highlighted.

Computer Activity

Note: If you don't have Word, use another word processor.

- Put standard heading at page top.
- Enter title, *Landforms,* underneath—bold, centered and underlined.
- Add a 3x5 table with the table tool . You'll need more than five rows, but we'll add those later.
- Add column headings in first row—*Landform, Example, Picture*. Move between cells with the tab (tab moves right; Shift+tab moves left), and from the last cell in a row to the next row.
- As students add landform types in column #1, discuss what they are. For column #2 *Examples*, use examples of landforms learned in class or from experience. Come up with one inside the US and one outside. Help only if needed.
- Do column #3, *Pictures*, last.
- When they get to the last cell in the last row, push tab to add a row.
- When finished, use internet search (i.e., Google) to find pictures of the landforms. Let them pause to enjoy the grandeur of nature in these pictures.
- Copy-paste image to correct cell. (Select only public pictures.)
- Check print preview before printing and resize images as needed to fit one page. (See following page)

Extensions

- Format column headings (shade row, bold text, enlarge font)
- Add a fourth column with a fact.

Troubleshooting Tips

- *I ran out of rows (add another by tabbing from the last cell in table)*
- *I can't print (Ctrl+P, file-print)*

LANDFORMS

Landform	Example	Picture
Forest	Amazon Rainforest Redwood forest	
Ocean	Pacific Ocean Indian Ocean	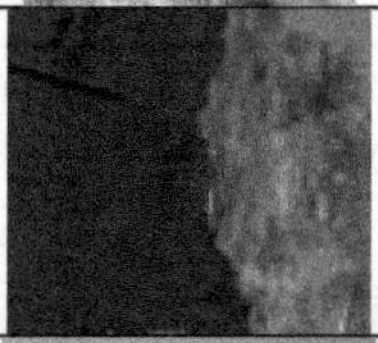
Desert	Sahara Desert Gobi Desert	
Rivers	Nile River Mississippi River	
Lake	Lake Michigan Lake Victoria	
Mountain	Mount Fuji Mount McKinley	
Plain	Savannah Great Plains	
Valley	Death Valley Nile Valley	
Glaciers	Antarctica Glaciers Alaska Glaciers	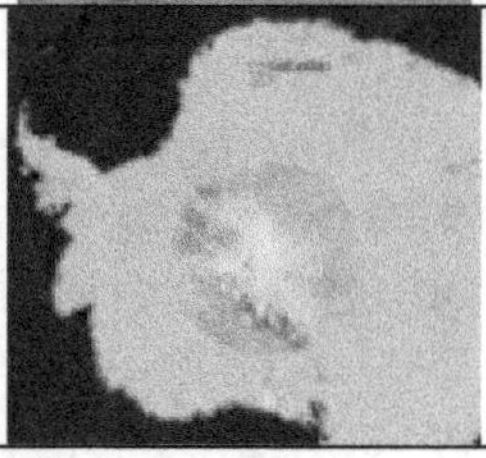

Subject #3: Geography

Project #47: Tour the World—with a PowerPoint Slideshow Use research done for Project #40 to create a slideshow, Wonders of Google Earth. Teach slideshow skills like adding slides/text/pictures, animation, transitions, auto-forward, backgrounds, adding music to multiple slides. Third graders may not be able to complete all skills.

Higher-order thinking skills	Technology-specific: PowerPoint	Subject Area/ Learning-specific	Standard: ISTE
Comprehension (interpret and understand)	*Basics, animations, transitions, adding items*	*Presentation skills, grammar and spelling, research and fluency*	*3a-d, 6a, 6c*

Grade level: 3-7
Prior knowledge: Intro to PowerPoint, Project 38 (Intro to Google Earth), Project 39 (Google Earth Board), Project 40 (Wonders of Google Earth)
Time required: 45 minutes, 4 sessions
Software required: PowerPoint (or your class slideshow tool), Google Earth
Vocabulary: multiple intelligences, slides, task pane, background, color schemes, font schemes, schemes

Lesson Description

- PowerPoint is a versatile presentation tool that integrates text, pictures, color, movement, and sound to grab an audience's attention.
- *Multiple Intelligences*, the term popularized by Howard Gardner, explains that students learn seven different ways. Slideshows use four of the seven.
- Students start PowerPoint as young as second grade and continue using it beyond HS. It's a favorite in the business world because it highlights important points.

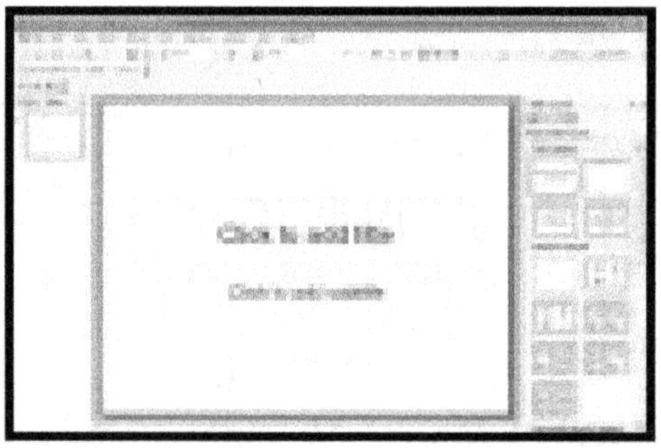

Computer Activity

Note: If you don't have PowerPoint, use another slideshow program.

- Introduce PowerPoint—its purpose, the basics, the page layout.
- Show samples of *Wonders of the World* slideshows from previous students.
- Open PowerPoint. Explain how slides are listed on the left, current slide shows in the middle and the task pane on the right (if needed).
- Create title slide with *Wonders of the World* as the heading and student name/teacher as subheading.
- Add eight slides with New Slide icon (not the drop down arrow). Select a background using the design menu. Left click to place the same background on all slides; right-click one design to place it on only one selected slide. From the Design tool ribbon, you can also adapt the color scheme.
- **Slide 2:** add Table of Contents with titles as listed on the storyboard (on next pages). These will be the titles placed at the top of each slide.
- **Slide 3:** Tell us what makes a location amazing. Consider what you heard in the presentations
- **Slide 4-6:** Each of these slides includes a location, where it is, and three facts (from the list collected

during the Google Earth Board—Project 39) about it (see inset).

- For each location slide, add an animated GIF and Google Earth picture about the location. Test the slideshow.

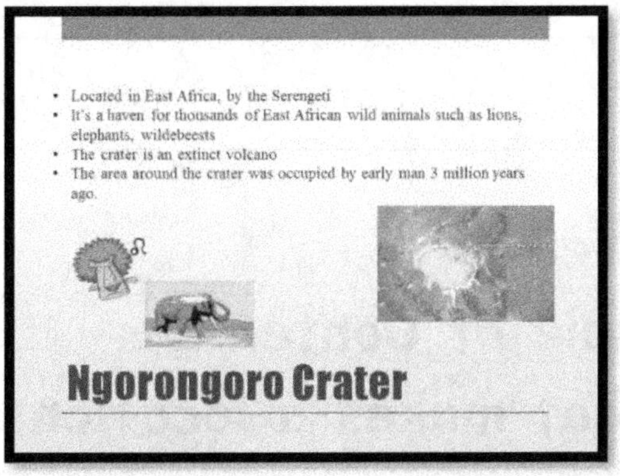

- **Slide 7:** List three locations you'd like to visit with a picture of each.
- **Slide 8:** Tell us what you learned about the world and geography. Is it not what you expected? Think about the presentations and draw some conclusions.
- **Slide 9:** *About the Author* is the title. Tell us something about yourself in the text box. This can be paragraph form or bullet list (see inset).
- Go to Transition menu to add a transition between slides. Explain what this is. Try different transitions before choosing. Select one for each slide. From this same ribbon, modify the speed of the transition, add a short sound (i.e., applause), and make slides automatically advance after eight seconds. This way, your slideshow will move forward automatically while you present.

- Go to the Animation menu item. An Animation is how the slide's text comes onto the screen. Try different animations. Pick the one you like. Select one for each slide.
- When completed, fill out the grading rubric (see following pages). Be sure you have all required elements.
- Don't print the sideshow.
- Students will present slideshows to the class. Play it on the class screen or Smartboard.
- Presenters must stay in sync with the show. Have them practice so they allow the right amount of time for each slide. Adjust the seconds required on the slide transition screen depending upon need.
- Make presentation grading rubric available early so students know what they will be judged on.

Extensions

- Add custom motion paths to slides
- Add music that continues throughout slideshow (from a song of their choice).
- Add custom backgrounds to several slides through the 'format background' dialogue box (easiest way to find that is with a right click on the background). From here, you can add a picture, custom background and/or artistic effect to the picture. Students love adding their school picture to About the Author' (see inset).
- Add links to Table of Contents entries to go directly to that slide.

Troubleshooting Tips

- *I can't see the animated GIF move (Shift+F5 starts the slideshow from the slide you're working on.)*

Slideshow: Wonders of Google Earth

Your name:____

Your teacher:____

Slide 1: Cover
Slide 2: Table of Contents
Slide 3: What makes a location amazing:

4. ________________________________
5. ________________________________
6. ________________________________

Slide 4: First of 3 locations (include map of location):

4. ____________________(Where is it located)
5. ____________________(1st amazing fact)
6. ____________________(2nd amazing fact)
7. ____________________(3rd amazing fact)

Slide 5: Second of 3 locations (include map of location):

1. ____________________(Where is it located)
2. ____________________(1st amazing fact)
3. ____________________(2nd amazing fact)
4. ____________________(3rd amazing fact)

Slide 6: Third of 3 locations (include map of location):

1. ______________________(Where is it located)
2. ______________________(1st amazing fact)
3. ______________________(2nd amazing fact)
4. ______________________(3rd amazing fact)

Slide 7: Three other locations you'd like to visit:

1. ____________________________________
2. ____________________________________
3. ____________________________________

Slide 8: What you learned about the world, geography, etc.:

1. ____________________________________
2. ____________________________________
3. ____________________________________

Slide 9: About the Author

- Who you live with____________________
- Your favorite books__________________
- Your hobbies________________________
- Your goals for this year______________
- Your goals for the future_____________

WONDERS OF GOOGLE EARTH TOUR FACTS

LOCATION	IN TERESTING FACTS
Ayers Rock	❖ One of the oldest rocks on Earth. ❖ Perimeter is 5 miles ❖ Has a waterfall called Alice Springs ❖ Changes colors depending upon the time of day
Death Valley	❖ Record for highest temperature in the Western hemisphere—134 degrees ❖ Second hottest recorded temperature in the world ❖ Lowest spot in North America at 282 feet below sea level
Egyptian Pyramids	❖ Pyramid features are so large they can be seen from the Moon ❖ The oldest structures in existence ❖ They are oriented north-south ❖ There are around 110 Egyptian pyramids
Eiffel Tower	❖ Built in 1887; completed in 1889 for the World Fair ❖ 324 meters tall, made out of 9441 tons of wrought iron ❖ Repainted every 7 years; requires 50 tons of brown paint in 3 shades, darkest at bottom ❖ More than 200,000 people visited it during the World's Fair of 1889
Great African Rift	❖ Named by the 19th century British explorer John Walter Gregory ❖ 3700 miles long, extending from Jordan to South Africa ❖ Site of the oldest human remains (3.7 million year old Lucy)
Great Wall of China	❖ …isn't a continuous wall. Stretches 4,000 miles ❖ Guarded by 2-3 million soldiers ❖ Built 2,000 years ago by first emperor of China; rebuilt many times
Hagia Sophia	❖ 'Hagia Sophia' means the church of the old wisdom in Greek ❖ One of several great churches built by Constantine the Great in the 4th Century ❖ Started as a basilica, became a mosque and is now a museum
Istanbul	❖ First known as Byzantium and then Constantinople, now third largest city in the world ❖ Use to be the capital of the East Roman Empire and the Ottoman Empire ❖ Located in Turkey, its main religion is Islam
Leaning Tower of Pisa	❖ Took 177 years to build; started 1173 ❖ 55.86 m tall on one side and 56.7 m tall on the other; weighs about 14,500 tons ❖ Took 70 tons of dirt to stabilize the tower in May 2008 ❖ It has 294 steps
Madagascar	❖ Island created when it separated from India 80-100 million years ago ❖ 4th largest island in the world ❖ Unlike its neighbor Africa, there are no lions, giraffes, zebras, hippos here ❖ Home to 5% of the world's plants and animals
Mt. Everest	❖ Started growing about 60 million years ago ❖ 4000 people have attempted to climb it, but only 660 have succeeded. ❖ 142 people died attempting to climb Mt. Everest ❖ Rises a few millimeters each year due to geologic forces

Mt. St. Helens	❖ An active volcano in the Cascade range in the state of Washington ❖ It is young for a volcano, only about 40,000 years old ❖ Last erupted May 18, 1980, for 9 hours. ❖ Killed 57 people, destroyed 250 homes, 47 bridges, 15 miles of railway, 185 miles of highway
Ngorongoro Crater	❖ A haven for thousands of East African wild animals—lions, elephants, wildebeests, etc. ❖ The crater of an extinct volcano ❖ The area around the crater was occupied by early man 3 million years ago
Panama Canal	❖ Manmade passage across Panama that connects the Pacific and Atlantic Oceans ❖ Started by the French and finished by the Americans ❖ One of the largest and most difficult engineering projects ever undertaken
Red Sea	❖ Created from the movement of tectonic plates over 3 million years ago ❖ One of the most saline bodies of water in the world ❖ More than 1100 species of fish live here—10% of them found nowhere else
Ross Ice Shelf	❖ About the size of France with 90% of the floating ice below the water's surface ❖ Twice the size of Delaware ❖ Largest ice shelf in Antarctica, sits about 50 meters high from the water ❖ James Clark Ross discovered it in 1841 ❖ Ice Shelves are permanent floating ice sheets attached to land, fed by glaciers
San Andreas Fault	❖ Land along the fault moves about 2 inches a year, as fast as fingernails grow ❖ Extends 800 miles down California, from Salton Sea to San Francisco bay ❖ Renowned as future source of the 'Big One'—earthquake that will tear California apart
Siberia	❖ Occupies 77% of Russia's land and only 30% of its population ❖ The vast region covering almost all of northern Asia, now under Russian control ❖ Soviet Union (no longer a nation) operated labor camps here during the mid-1900's for millions of political refugees, making 'Siberia' synonymous with exile and punishment
Stonehenge	❖ Blocks weighed as much as 4 tons and were moved as far as 240 miles ❖ Built around 2500 B.C.E. ❖ Not actually a henge—based on construction
Straits of Gibraltar	❖ 22 miles wide ❖ separates Spain from Morocco ❖ Strait of Gibraltar closed about 6 million years ago and reopened a million years later
Suez Canal	❖ Canal is 26 feet deep ❖ Opened in November 1869 ❖ Owned by an Egyptian company
Taj Mahal	❖ 5th of the 7 Wonders of the World ❖ Built by the Muslim Emperor Shah Jahan in memory of his wife ❖ Took 22 years to make
Tierra del Fuego	❖ Tierra del Fuego is Spanish for "Land of Fire" ❖ Archipelago west of South America; extends to Strait of Magellan and Cape Horn ❖ Main island of the archipelago is also called Tierra del Fuego
Victoria Falls	❖ Twice the height of Niagara Falls ❖ Called the "Smoke that Thunders" ❖ Makes the largest curtain of water in the world ❖ 1 mile wide; 360 feet tall

SLIDESHOW GRADING RUBRIC

*Name*____________________ *Teacher*__________________

Here's a list of skills required in your PowerPoint project. Check off those that you've included. Then, add those that you've missed. Turn in with your presentation.

- Title slide ____________________
- Table of Contents ____________________
- The end slide ____________________
- Each slide has a background ____________________
- Each slide has title ____________________
- Each location slide has 3 facts and location ____________________
- Each slide has picture ____________________
- Each slide has GIF ____________________
- No spelling/grammar errors ____________________
- 5 animations ____________________
- 5 transitions ____________________
- Slides auto-advance at reasonable speed ____________________
- Class presentation ____________________
    i. Talk to audience ____________________
    ii. Introduce yourself and topic ____________________
    iii. Speak loud enough ____________________
    iv. No 'umms', slang or stuttering ____________________
    v. Slide show progresses smoothly ____________________
    vi. Student understands locations ____________________
    vii. Student can answer questions ____________________
- **Custom background* ____________________
- *Custom animation* ____________________
- *Custom music* ____________________

**Italics indicate extra credit items*

Subject #3: Geography

Project #48: Sponge Activities for Geography. Introduce students to web-based geography activities that can be done in five or ten minutes between lessons, before lunch, in free time. I include five in this lesson.

Higher-order thinking skills	Technology-specific:	Subject Area/ Learning-specific	Standard: ISTE
Applying—use concepts in new situations	*Use technology to broaden subject matter competency, learn the basics of internet*	*Reinforce spelling, class word lists*	*3a, 3d*

Grade level: 2-8
Prior knowledge: Project 99 (Internet Basx)—from Book II (if you have it)
Time required: 5-10 minutes
Software required: Google Earth
Vocabulary: administrivia, website, structure, geography, favorites, hits

Lesson Description

- What's a sponge activity? Originally used by Madeline Hunter, a "sponge" is an activity designed to produce learning during the times taken up by "administrivia." They stem from Hunter's teaching philosophy that there should be no wasted moments in her classroom.
- Each of these websites offers quick activities for students, taking 5-10 minutes.

Computer Activity

- Give students a list of world locations in the news. Let them lose on Google Earth. Have them find the spots and read what people all over the world have uploaded about the location.
- Geography matching games
- MathTrail--mix math and geography
- Quizzity–geography quiz game
- Geogreeting—find letters in man-made and natural structures around the world
- Geography games—Nat'l Geographic
- Seterra–geography games
- Geonet

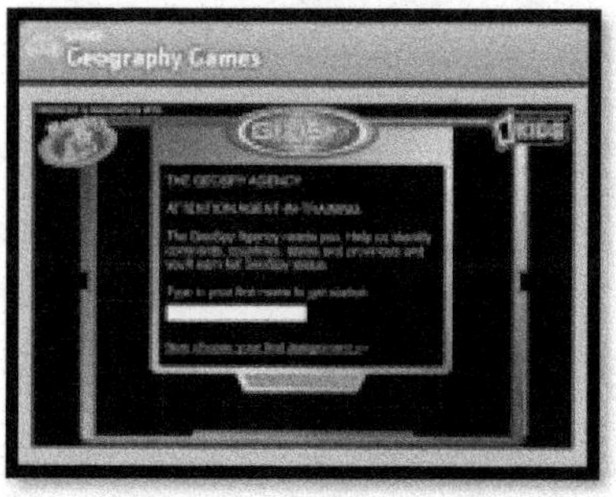

Extensions

- Add these websites to favorites to be used more quickly

Troubleshooting Tips

- *I get a list of hits—not the site (did you type the address into the search bar by accident, rather than the address bar?)*

Subject #4: History

Project #49: California Missions Magazine in Publisher. Create a California Mission (or any other classroom topic) magazine in MS Publisher. Include a cover, table of contents, banner heading, border, text boxes with researched data, works cited page, pictures, and items from the design gallery. This authentic project also teaches students desktop publishing basics they can use throughout school.

Higher-order thinking skills	Technology-specific:	Subject Area/ Learning-specific	Standard: ISTE
Applying info, remembering	*Citations from the internet Using Publisher*	*Cultures, history, geography, spelling, grammar*	*3a-d*

Grade level: 4-6
Prior knowledge: Project 22 or 30 (Publisher flier or cover page), Project 52 (Indigenous Cultures Magazine)
Time required: 45 minutes, 4 sessions
Software required: Publisher (or your class DTP tool)
Vocabulary: citations, design gallery, quick publications, pull quote, sidebar, auto shapes, copyright, bullets, banner heading, clipboard

Lesson Description

- Students make a California Missions magazine with a Table of Contents, a page for each topic covered in the Contents page, a Works Cited page to credit each website visited for bullet points and pictures, and a collage of pictures at the end.
- For grades 5-6, this can cover any topic that collaborates with curriculum.

Computer Activity

Note: If you don't have Publisher, use another DTP tool (like Canva).

- Show samples of magazines or prior year's projects.
- Open Publisher. Use Quick Publications (as done for fliers and cover pages in prior projects).

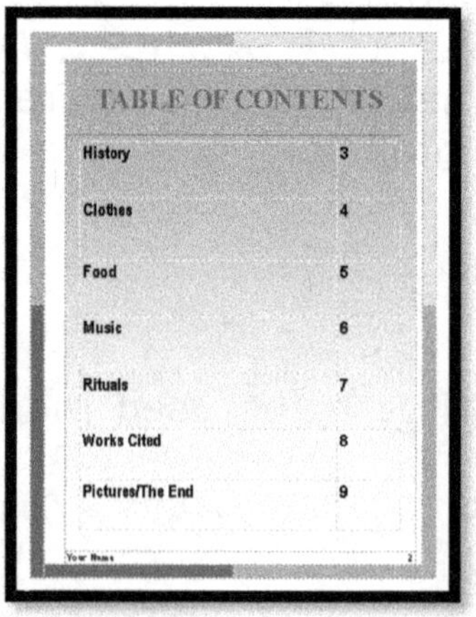

- Adjust color and font schemes to reflect student's vision of California Missions. Add the Mission name. Add student name and teacher name below (as shown on inset).
- Add eight more pages. Explain what the blue border means (this is a print border. All items except the border must stay inside of it to insure they are printed correctly)
- Add footer with student name and page #.
- Page 2: Add Table of Contents (insert-Building Blocks-Page Parts-Table of Contents). Add topics that fit your curriculum needs. Title should be font size 26, entries font size 18. Show students how to use tab to move between cells.
- Page 3: Add a map of California Missions. Put a star where student's mission is located (insert-shapes-stars and

banners). Use paint bucket fill to make star stand out.

- Page 3-8: Add a border (insert-borders). Resize border to avoid footer. Show students how to copy-paste border to pages 4-9. Explain how a copied item remains on the clipboard to be used wherever they want to paste it. Show them how to use move tool to adjust position. Explain difference between 'move tool' and 'resize tool'. Be sure footer shows above or below border. Add a banner heading (explain what a 'banner heading' is) with Wordart and copy-paste to pages 4-8; edit text to match the page's topic, per table of contents.
- Page 3-7: Add sidebar to each page (insert-building blocks-page parts- sidebar) as a bullet list of five 'fast facts' discussed in class about the page topic. Students should list these from memory or go over them as a group.
- Page 3-7: Include a quote (using Publisher's 'pull quote' item) on the page topic (see inset). Use the list of resources on the next page to find quotes about Missions. Use the Websites at end of book for resources on other topics.

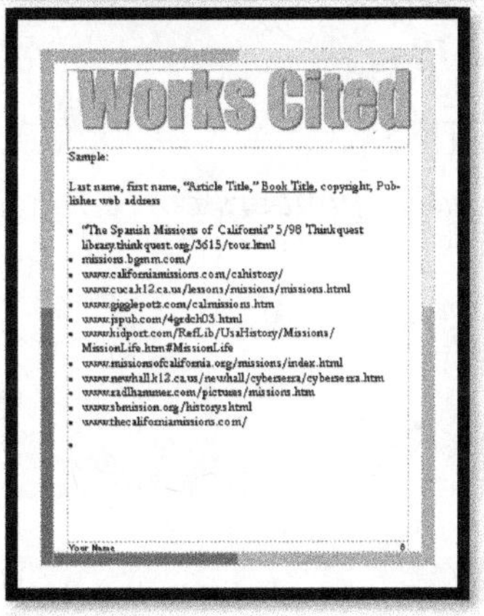
Works Cited

Sample:

Last name, first name, "Article Title," Book Title, copyright, Publisher web address

- "The Spanish Missions of California" 5/98 Thinkquest library.thinkquest.org/3615/tour.html
- missions.bgmm.com/
- www.californiamissions.com/cahistory/
- www.cuca.k12.ca.us/lessons/missions/missions.html
- www.gigglepotz.com/calmissions.htm
- www.jspub.com/4grdch03.html
- www.kidport.com/RefLib/UsaHistory/Missions/MissionLife.htm#MissionLife
- www.missionsofcalifornia.org/missions/index.html
- www.newhall.k12.ca.us/newhall/cyberserra/cyberserra.htm
- www.radlhammer.com/pictures/missions.htm
- www.sbmission.org/history.shtml
- www.thecaliforniamissions.com/

Your Name 8

- Page 3-7: Add pictures to fill out page.
- Page 8: List your resources. Bullet list each website visited (see inset). Fourth grade: Modify MLA format. Include:
  - Blue bar title in quotes
  - Website address
  - Copyright, where available

Grades 5-6: Use MLA citation guidelines.

- Page 9: Add a collage of themed pictures. Layer 'The End' in Wordart (see inset) over pictures. Show students how to layer items.

Extensions

- Have all students follow MLA format for the 'Works Cited' page.
- Have students link each Table of Contents entry to its page and publish magazine as pdf and/or Google Doc.

Troubleshooting Tips

1. My bullets disappeared.

(Use the bullet tool on the toolbar.)

DTP Mission Research

Grading Rubric

*Your name:*____

*Teacher:*____

4. Title Page	2 points___
a. *Mission's full name in large font*	________
b. *Your name, teacher in smaller font*	________
c. *Picture of your mission*	________
d. *Grammar and spelling*	________
5. Table of Contents	3 points___
a. *All topics listed, page numbers correct*	________
b. *No white space*	________
c. *Fonts/sizes correct*	________
d. *Spelling correct*	________
6. Individual Pages	6 points___
a. *Border*	________
b. *Banner heading*	________
c. *Bullet list and sidebar*	________
d. *Correct grammar*	________
e. *No slang*	________
f. *Correct spelling*	________
g. *3-4 pictures, from the era*	________
h. *Pictures resized correctly*	________
i. *Footer with your name, page*	________
7. Works Cited Page	3 points___
a. *'Blue bar' title*	________
b. *Web address*	________
c. *Copyright date (if available)*	________
8. The End Page	3 points___
a. *'The End' in WordArt*	________
b. *'The End' layered over pics*	________
c. *No white space (filled with pictures)*	________
9. Overall Professional Look	3 points___

Subject #4: History

Project #50: American Revolution Magazine in Publisher. Similar to #49, but longer with more design elements. This also includes a diagram for organizing ideas, a table of data, a timeline of events (which can also be used as a separate project). Very impressive when completed. You might prefer doing this in a group—it's a fairly involved project.

Higher-order thinking skills	Technology-specific:	Subject Area/ Learning-specific	Standard: ISTE
Integrate knowledge, understand	*Basic/Intermediate, use of creative content and Design Gallery*	*History, grammar, spelling*	*3a-d*

Grade level: 5-8
Prior knowledge: Project 49 (California Missions Magazine; suggested: Project 52 (Indigenous Cultures Magazine)
Time required: 4 weeks (research done outside of technology class)
Software required: Publisher (or your class DTP tool)
Vocabulary: Design Gallery, text boxes, call outs, auto shapes, schemes,

Lesson Description

- Students communicate involved ideas with text, pictures, colors and an attractive layout.
- This summative project reinforces class discussion on the American Revolution while it teaches advanced desktop publishing skills. It fosters curiosity about historic events while learning to create a professional, sophiscated project suitable for MS and HS.

- Each page is designed to cover a different technology skill set, reinforcing learning in an authentic and cognitive manner.
- Because of the project's detail, you might want students to work in teams.

Computer Activity

Note: If you don't have Publisher, use another DTP program (like Canva).

- Open Publisher. Use Quick Publications (as students have done for fliers and cover pages in prior projects).
- Adjust color and font schemes to reflect student's vision of the magazine. Add title, student name and teacher (as shown in inset).
- Add 13 pages. Add footer with student name and page #. Discuss the meaning of 'footer' and why we use them.

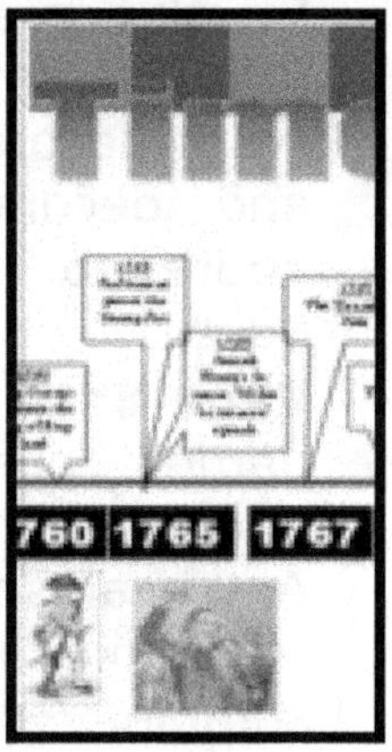

- **Page 2:** Add Table of Contents (insert-building blocks—page parts—Table of Contents). Add topics as shown on following pages or adapt to suit your needs. Title should be font size 26, entries font 18.

- **Page 3-10:** Add a border (add to page 3 and copy-paste to pages 4-10 as was done in #49). Add a WordArt banner heading at top with page name (add to page 3, copy-paste to pages 4-10 and edit text to reflect the unique page name). Pick a decorative item from Building Blocks—Borders and Accents and layer it under the page title. Use the same one for each page to add continuity to the magazine.
- **Page 3:** Photo Journal. Add a caption to each picture. All white space should be filled.
- **Page 4-5:** A Timeline of events. Use an autoshape line for the timeline, filled text boxes for the dates, and call-outs above the timeline for 10-13 events. Add pictures below the timeline to highlight important events. See example for detail.
- **Page 6-7, 11-12:** Discuss the British and American parts in the revolution, the effects of the Revolution and inventions resulting from the Revolution. Use text boxes (with decorative borders), pictures and decorative items. Add one quote to each page using pull quotes.
- **Page 8:** Use a table to discuss the name, position, event and a quotation of famous British and American soldiers. Format the table to make titles stand out. See sample.
- **Page 9:** Use a graphic organizer (create in MS Word using SmartArt and copy-paste) to discuss the Pros and Cons of the Revolution. See sample.
- **Page 10:** Find a primary source document from this period. Copy-paste it into the magazine. Be sure to give credit to the source.
- Page 13: Write 'The End' in WordArt.
- See samples following this project lesson.

Extensions

- As an alternative, students can create a magazine about world revolutions or another topic you are discussing in your classroom.
- Add more primary source documents.
- Have students follow standard MLA format for the 'Works Cited' page.

Troubleshooting Tips

1. *Everyone in the group has their own magazine. How do we merge them? (Create one master. Bring that one up on the computer as well as all the segments. Copy-paste from a segment to the master. You'll find this easy to do in Publisher. Or, complete all articles using Google Docs, then copy-paste information to the Publisher document.)*
2. *We want to share the magazine on the class blog, but the internet doesn't like Publisher files. What can we do? (Save as a pdf and upload. Great idea to share work online!)*

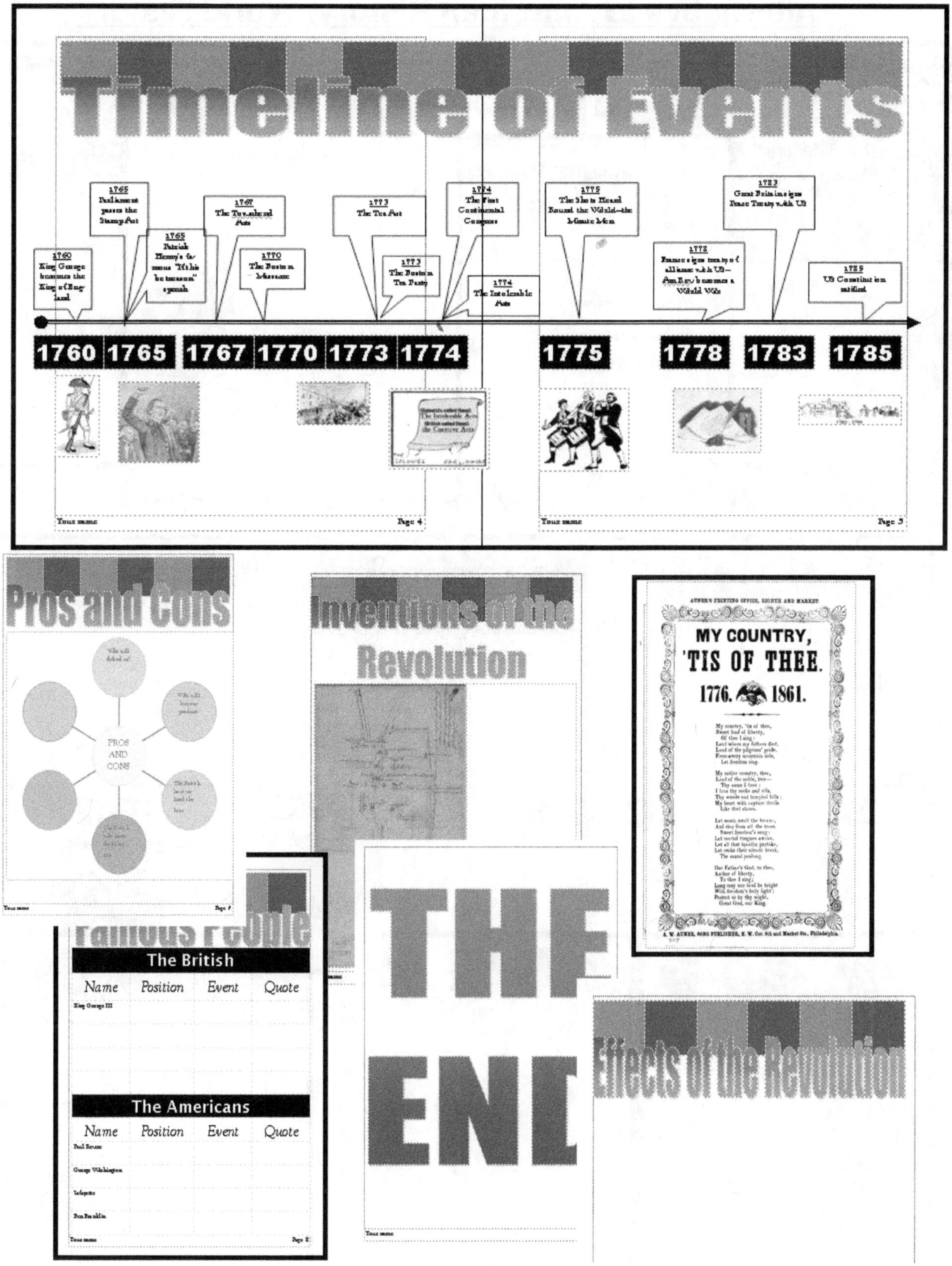
Timeline of Events
1760
1765
1767
1770
1773
1774
1775
1778
1783
1785
Pros and Cons
Inventions of the Revolution
MY COUNTRY,
'TIS OF THEE.
1776. 1861.
The British
Name Position Event Quote
The Americans
Name Position Event Quote
THE
END
Effects of the Revolution

Alternative to American History: World History

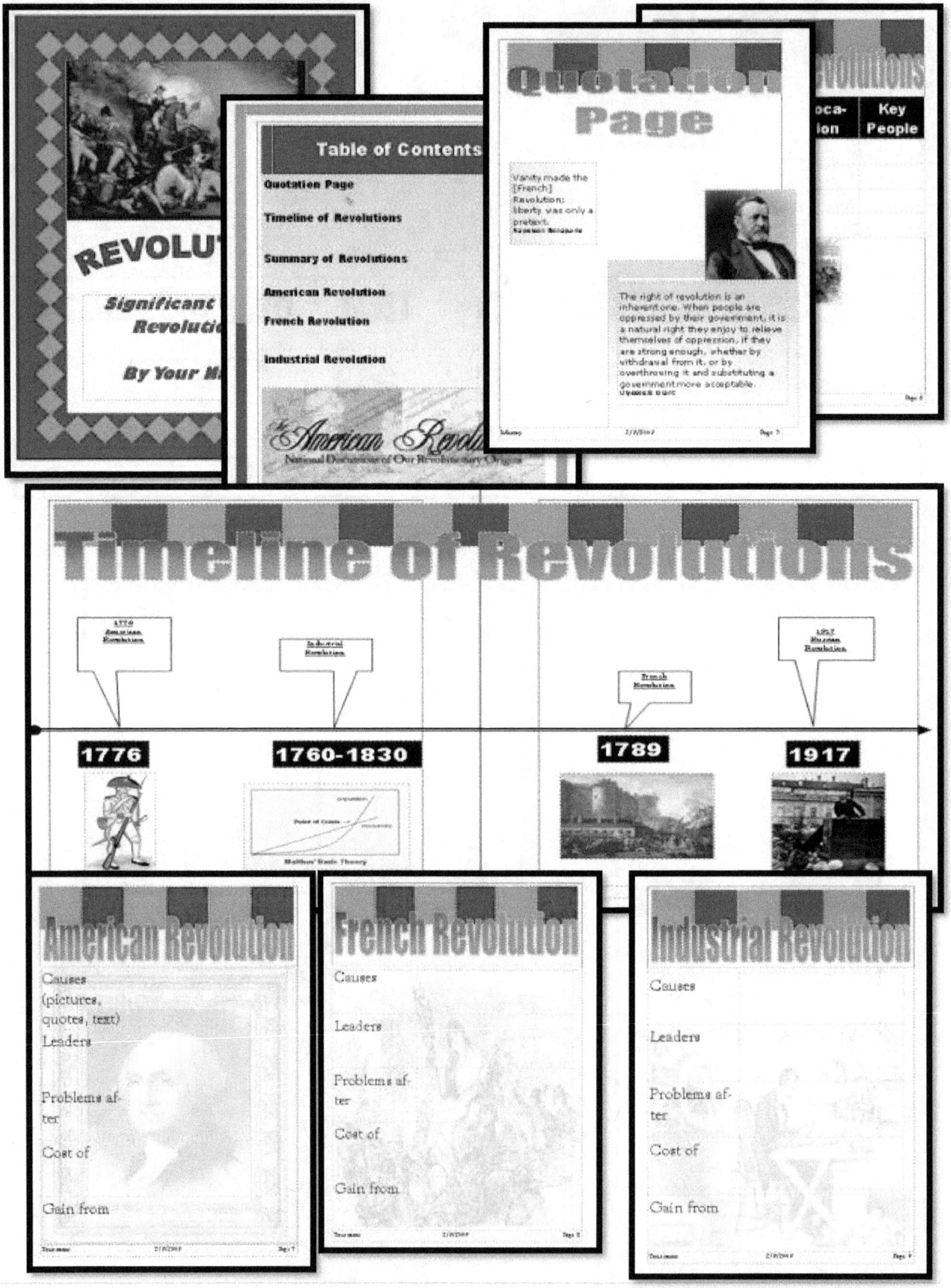

Subject #4: History

Project #51: This Day in History/This Day in My Life. Students create a tri-fold brochure, scaffolding on previous tech knowledge, to compare what was happening in their life when something else significant was happening around the world. For example, the student went to Disneyland when Dolly the Sheep was cloned. Curiosity is fostered and global citizenship encouraged as students use templates, add text, pictures, a time line, and design elements. This is a popular project with students—who are always amazed at what happened around the world—and parents.

Higher-order thinking skills	Technology-specific:	Subject Area/ Learning-specific	Standard: ISTE
Integrate knowledge, understand	*Basic/Intermediate, use of creative content and Design Gallery*	*History, grammar, spelling*	*3a-d*

Grade level: 4-6
Prior knowledge: 3-4 projects in Publisher to develop knowledge of its capabilities
Time required: 45 minutes, 4 sessions
Software required: Publisher (or your class DTP tool)
Vocabulary: click, drag-and-drop, brochure, color block, watermark, washout, order, send to back

Lesson Description

- Trifold brochures are used for a variety of educational reasons. Their simple design and snapshot approach makes them easy to read and keep for reference. Plus, a cornerstone of their form is the multi-intelligence mix of text, pictures, and colors.

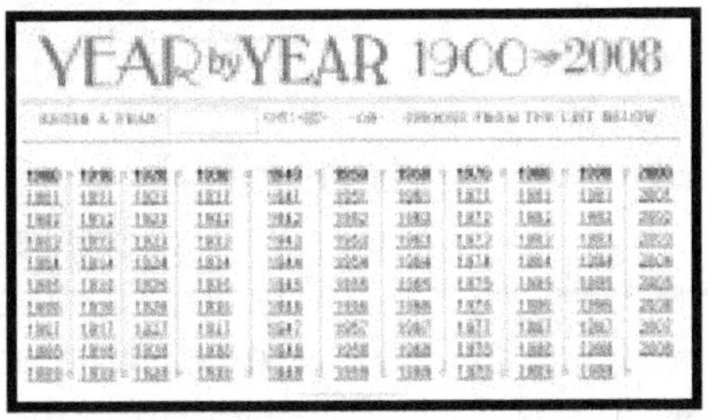

- The brochure should reflect creativity, solid design principles, and an interdisciplinary array of skills as students develop a cognitive understanding of themselves as global citizens.

Computer Activity

Note: If you don't have Publisher, use another DTP alternative (like Canva).

- Before starting, show students how a trifold works. People look first at the cover—so this must be enticing and splashy. They then flip the brochure over. The back should incorporate color, pictures and enough text to communicate the message. By now, the viewer must be willing to take the plunge and open the trifold. Once they've done this, the three panels on page 2 must work together to tell the story.
- Spend the first class collecting one event in world history for each year in students' life.
- Then, have students collect one event from each year of their life. Talk to parents and family members—what was a major event each year the student was alive.
- Open Publisher. Click on brochures. Any will do because we will delete everything on it.
- Click and drag a box around the contents of Page 1. Delete. Repeat on page 2.
- Page 1: Panel one—insert a text box that covers the bottom half of the panel. Add *This Day in History,*

student name and teacher name (on separate lines), font size 36, centered, bold.

- Copy the text box and paste into Panel three. Edit text to read, *This Day in My Life.* Leave the other lines unedited.

- Add color block on top half of panel one (insert- shapes—basic shapes—rectangle). Fill it with the paint bucket in a color of your choice.
- Copy-paste the color block onto the top of Panel three and two. Resize so it fills the full length of Panel two.
- Have students layer their picture over the color block on Panel three.
- Search Google images for four pictures of historic events researched by students. Arrange three onto Panel two and one at top of Panel three.
- Page 2: Insert a timeline (insert-shapes-line) Use the shift key to drag the line across the page straight.

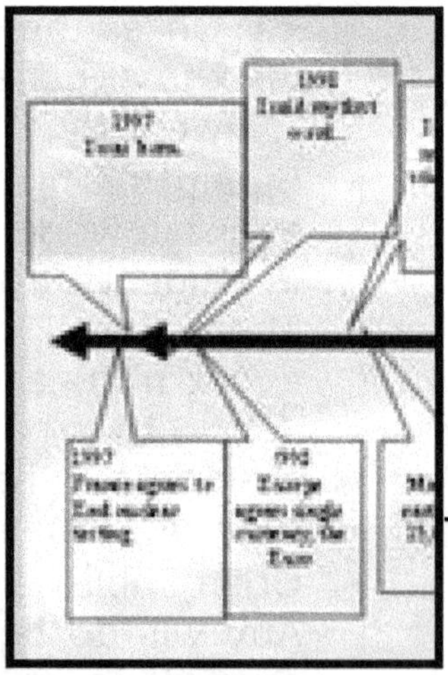

- Insert a call-out (insert-shapes-callouts). Size it so that three can fit to a panel. Now copy-paste nine above and nine below the line. Arrange so that the tips of two meet on the timeline (see example).
- Starting at the left, add the date and event for all nine historic events that occurred during the student's life above the timeline. Add the nine life events below the line. Be sure that events in matching years match up.
- Next, student copy their picture from Page one and paste it onto Page two. Anywhere is fine, because we are going to format it.
- Enlarge picture so it fills page. Bring up 'Format Picture' dialogue box (right click). On the 'picture' tab, change automatic to washout. Close dialogue box.
- Right click picture, select order, send to back. Student picture should now be behind the timeline and look like a watermark.
- When student finishes, have them complete the rubric (see next pages) checklist to make sure they have all required elements. Print; save to student folder; save-as to flash drive.

Extensions

- Add pictures of events on timeline page. Resize so they fit nicely.
- Color the callouts with the paint bucket fill. Color font. Change border around callouts.
- To tilt pictures, click green dot at top and drag image to preferred angle.
- Add a border around page two, and/or around Panel 1/ 3 on Page 1.

Troubleshooting Tips

- *I can't see my picture on Pg. 2 (Some don't show up well on the monitors, but it will when printed.)*
- *I forgot my list of historic events (Have students borrow from a different class, with the promise they will bring their own the following week.)*

Trifold Brochure
Grading Rubric

Your name: ______________________________

Your homeroom teacher: ______________________________

- Title Page (2 title pages) — **6 points**
  - *Large font* ______
  - *Your name and class in smaller font* ______
  - *Picture/color block fills white space* ______
  - *Border* ______
  - *Grammar and spelling* ______
- Collage — **2 points**
  - *3 pictures of world events* ______
  - *No white space (use color block)* ______
- Page Two — **10 points**
  - *Watermark background* ______
  - *Border around full page* ______
  - *Timeline with18 callouts* ______
  - *Events are significant and important* ______
  - *Spell-check* ______
  - *Grammar check* ______
  - *Page filled* ______
- Overall Professional Look — **2 points**

How I grade myself: ______________________________

Explain: ______________________________

____

This Day in My Life
By Your Name
Your Teacher
This Day in History
By Your Name
Your Teacher

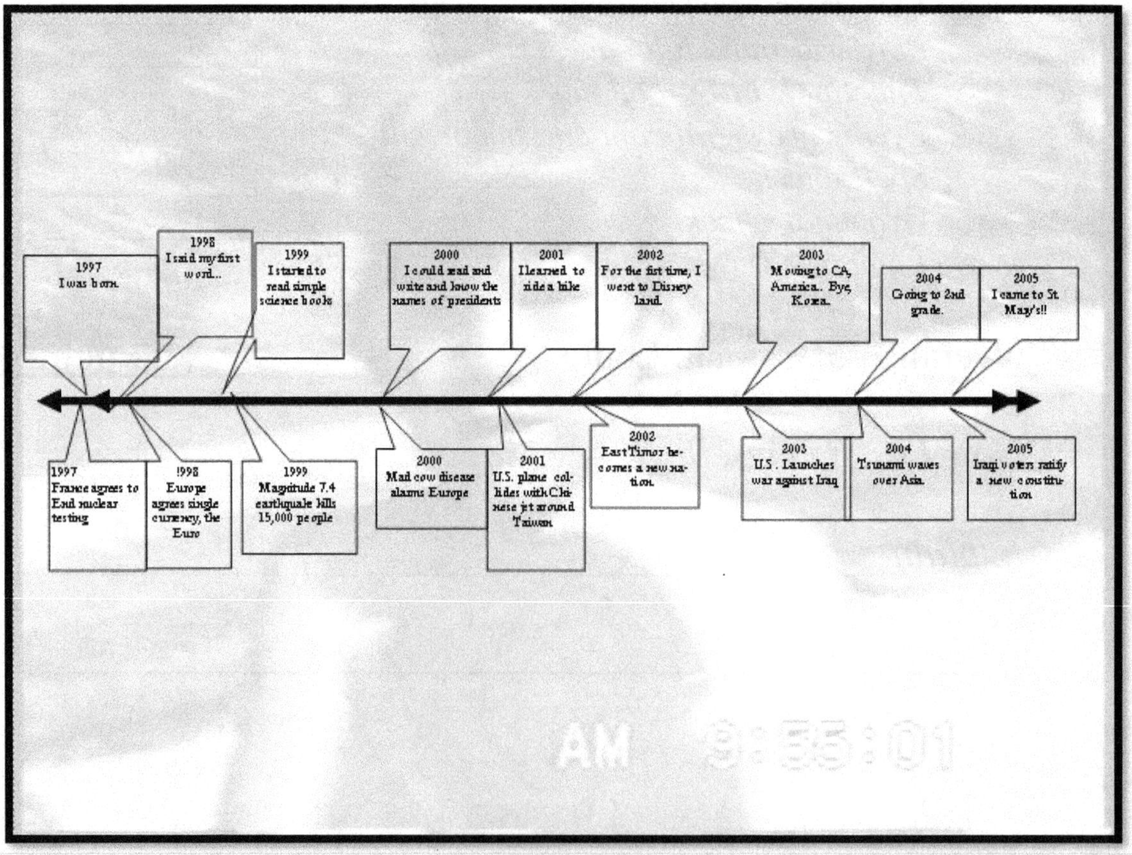
1997
I was born.
1998
I said my first word...
1999
I started to read simple science books
2000
I could read and write and know the names of presidents
2001
I learned to ride a bike
2002
For the fist time, I went to Disney-land.
2003
Moving to CA, America.. Bye, Korea.
2004
Going to 2nd grade.
2005
I came to St. Mary's!!
1997
France agrees to End nuclear testing
1998
Europe agrees single currency, the Euro
1999
Magnitude 7.4 earthquake kills 15,000 people
2000
Mad cow disease alarms Europe
2001
U.S. plane col-lides with Chi-nese jet around Taiwan
2002
East Timor be-comes a new na-tion.
2003
U.S. Launches war against Iraq
2004
Tsunami waves over Asia.
2005
Iraqi voters ratify a new constitu-tion
AM 9:55:01

Subject #4: History

Project #52: Indigenous Cultures Magazine in Publisher. This project introduces the basics of magazine creation in Publisher while students engage in inquiry-based learning that incorporates discovery and fosters curiosity. The project includes a cover, table of contents, border, map, banner title, five fast facts and pictures. This is an easy project that always comes out nicely for learners.

Higher-order thinking skills	Technology-specific:	Subject Area/ Learning-specific	Standard: ISTE
Evaluating /remembering information	*Citations from the internet Using Publisher*	*Cultures, history, geography, spelling, grammar*	*6a-d*

Grade level: 3
Prior knowledge: Project 30: Cover Page in Publisher, Project 99 (from Book II of this collection)
Time required: 45 minutes
Software required: MS Publisher (or your class DTP tool)
Vocabulary: schemes, design gallery, table of contents, font, border, .jpg, copy-paste, WordArt, collage

Lesson Description

- Create a Publisher magazine that enables students to communicate involved ideas with text, pictures, colors. The book layout makes it easy to design a two-page spread (as when you open a magazine).
- Students understand that writing strategies include more than text, that active learning includes the visual multi-intelligences as much as the written.
- The project introduces design elements of desktop publishing. Each page requires different critical thinking skills as it collaborates with classroom inquiry into the focus area.

Computer Activity

Note: If you don't have Publisher, use another DTP alternative (like Canva).

- Open Publisher. Start with the cover page by using Quick Publications (as students have done for fliers and cover pages in prior projects).
- Adjust color and font schemes to reflect student's vision of indigenous cultures. Add the title, *But I Was Here First*, student name and teacher name.
- Add 5 pages. Add footer with student name and page #. Discuss the meaning of 'footer' and why we use them.
- **Page 2:** Add Table of Contents (insert-building blocks—page parts—Table of Contents). Resize so

it fits the page, but doesn't go outside of blue print border. Discuss what the 'print border' is and why. Add topics as shown on following page or adapt to suit class needs. Title should be font size 26, entries font 18. Delete unused table rows. If there's room at the page bottom, add pictures on the cultures discussed in the magazine.

- **Page 3-5:** Add a border (add to page 3, resize if needed, and copy-paste to pages 4-5 as was done in #49). Add a WordArt banner heading at top with page name (add to page 3, resize as needed, copy-paste to pages 4-5 and edit text to reflect the unique page name).
- **Page 3-5:** Add a world map (resized to fit the space available at the page's bottom). Add a star (insert-shapes-stars) to the map to show where the culture being discussed is located. Fill the star with the paint bucket. Copy-paste the map also to pages 4 and 5 but adjust the position of the star.
- **Page 3-5:** Add two pictures to each page that incorporate discovery about the topic and communicate the student's ideas. Resize to fit (see sample).
- **Pages 3-5:** Add a text box. Add five fast facts about the topic. These should come from classroom discussion, not in-class research. Discuss this with students, even develop two-three with them so they can see how to be inquirers and engage in their own learning. If they are having difficulty, allow them to work with their neighbor.
- **Page 6:** Add a collage of pictures about all three cultures. Fill the page so no white space shows. Overlay 'The End' in WordArt.

Extensions

- Add a page with websites where students can go to research their topics.
- If you have a blog, have students post their favorite websites.

Troubleshooting Tips

- *My pages show a # in the footer, not the page number. (When you're in the footer toolbar, push the # sign from the ribbon. You probably used # over the 3.)*

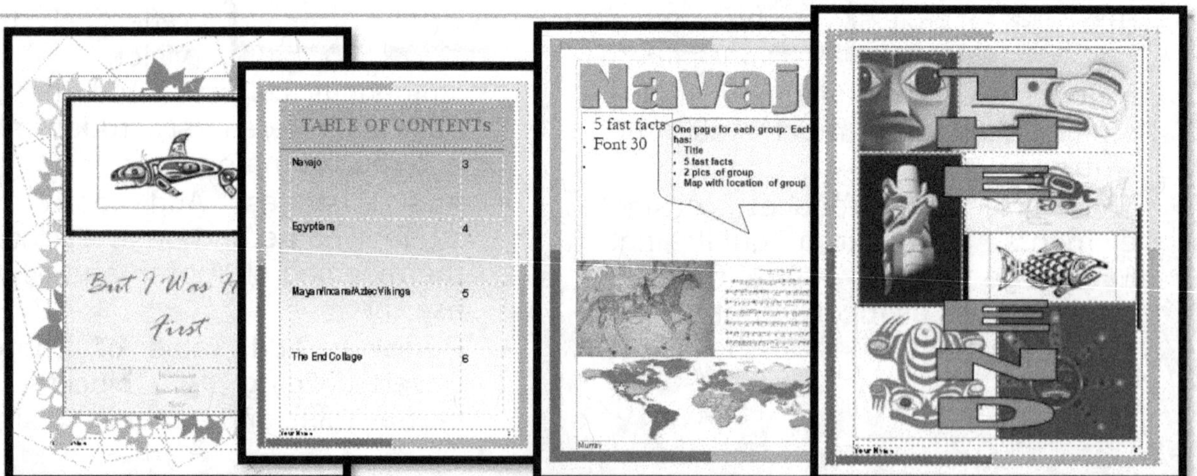

'But I Was Here First' Grading Rubric

*Your name:*____

*Teacher:*____

- **Title Page** — **2 points**
  - *Title in large font* __________
  - *Your name in smaller font* __________
  - *Picture related to topic* __________
- **Table of Contents** — **4 points**
  - *Decorative border* __________
  - *All topics listed* __________
  - *Page numbers match magazine* __________
  - *Spell-check, grammar check* __________
  - *Extra rows deleted* __________
  - *No white space* __________
- **Magazine Content Pages** — **4 points**
  - *Border on each page* __________
  - *WordArt title at top of page* __________
  - *Five fast facts* __________
  - *Map with star* __________
  - *Two pictures on topic* __________
  - *Footer with your name, page* __________
- **The End Page** — **4 points**
  - *The End in Word Art* __________
  - *The End layered over pictures* __________
  - *Picture Collage* __________
- **Overall Professional Look** — **3 points**
- **Overall Grammar/spelling** — **3 points**

Subject #4: History

Project #53: A Colonization Brochure in Publisher. Create a trifold brochure to support class inquiry into colonization or another unit. This project integrates research with tech presentation of thoughts and ideas, a true summative exercise that fosters curiosity and creativity. It encourages student interaction with material in the stimulating learning environment of technology and desktop publishing.

Higher-order thinking skills	Technology-specific:	Subject Area/ Learning-specific	Standard: ISTE
Integrate knowledge, understand	*Basic/Intermediate, use of creative content and Design Gallery*	*History, grammar, spelling*	*3.b, 3.c*

Grade level: 5
Prior knowledge: Project 51: This Day in My Life
Time required: 45 minutes, 4 sessions
Software required: Publisher (or your class DTP tool)
Vocabulary: click, drag-and-drop, brochure, color block, watermark, washout, order, send to back, layer, overflow, panel, sepia, grayscale

Lesson Description

- Trifold brochures are used for a variety of educational reasons. Their simple design and snapshot approach make them easy to read, fold and keep for reference. Plus, a cornerstone of their form is the multi-intelligence mix of text, pictures, and colors.
- This brochure should reflect creativity, solid design principles, consistency in the selection of fonts, sizes, colors.

Computer Activity

Note: If you don't have Publisher, use another DTP alternative (like Canva).

- Before starting, show students how a trifold works. People look first at the cover—so this must be enticing and splashy. They then flip the brochure over. The back should incorporate color, pictures and enough text to communicate the message. By now, the viewer must be willing to take the plunge and open the trifold. Once they've done this, the three panels on page 2 must work together to tell the story.

- Open Publisher. Click on brochures. Have students select one with a design and layout they like.
- **Page 1:** Panel three—This is the cover and should have only three items on it: the title, a picture and student name/teacher (see inset). The rest of the cover is design elements (color blocks, decorative bars, etc.) Have students delete all other place savers and adapt the template to this layout (as shown in inset). Title should be prominent, either a large font or Word Art. Picture should be topic-specific.
- **Page 1:** Panel two—This is the back flap—what viewers will see second. Add a map or a catchy picture (sample shows a watermark) and limited text, but enough to draw the viewer in.
- **Page 1:** Panel one—Put the pithiest question here, with at least one picture.

- **Page 2:** Add the balance of the information on this topic to these three panels. This is the meat of the brochure (see next page). Mix in pictures, color blocks, Design Gallery elements to spice up the information.
- Throughout brochure, titles should match in font, size, and color. They should be larger and more prominent than other text on the page, but consistent from one panel to the next. Text of articles should match in font, font size, font color and line spacing.

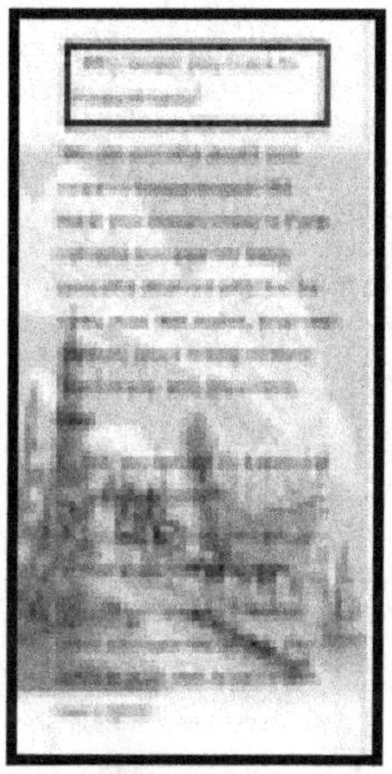

- Pictures must fit the era. Adjust them to sepia or grayscale if necessary.
- Delete all extraneous place savers and elements not necessary to student brochure.
- When student has completed the project, have them fill out the rubric (see next pages) checklist to make sure they have all required elements. Print brochure. Stable the top and bottom with white sides together. Fold into a trifold design.

Save to student network folder; save-as to flash drive

Extensions

- If this project comes after the classroom unit on the topic, challenge students to answer the essential questions from memory. Think about what they learned in class and use that information. Communicate your high expectations that they exhibit individual accountability for exploration into this subject. If technology lab is only once a week, this avoids the problem, *I forgot my notes.* And it reinforces learning by forcing them to remember and relate—essential Higher Order Thinking Skills.
- Create a watermark picture. Place it behind the text on Page 1, panel 1 (see sample below).

Troubleshooting Tips

- *My text disappeared. I'm typing, but nothing's happening! (Do you see an 'A' under the text box? This means the text box is too small for the inputted text. Resize it and all your typing will reappear.)*

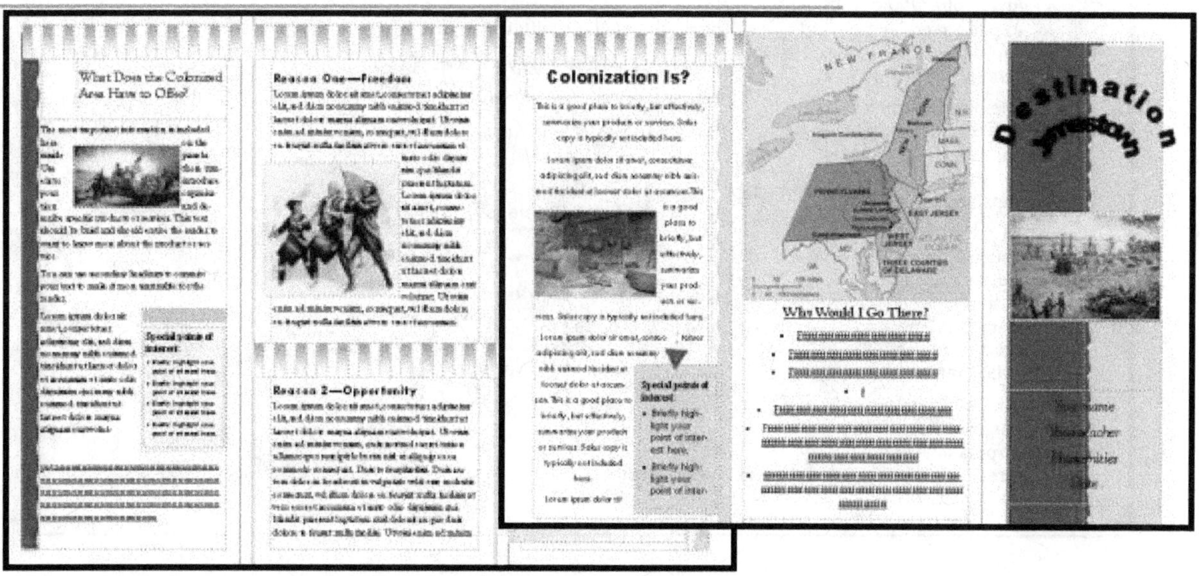

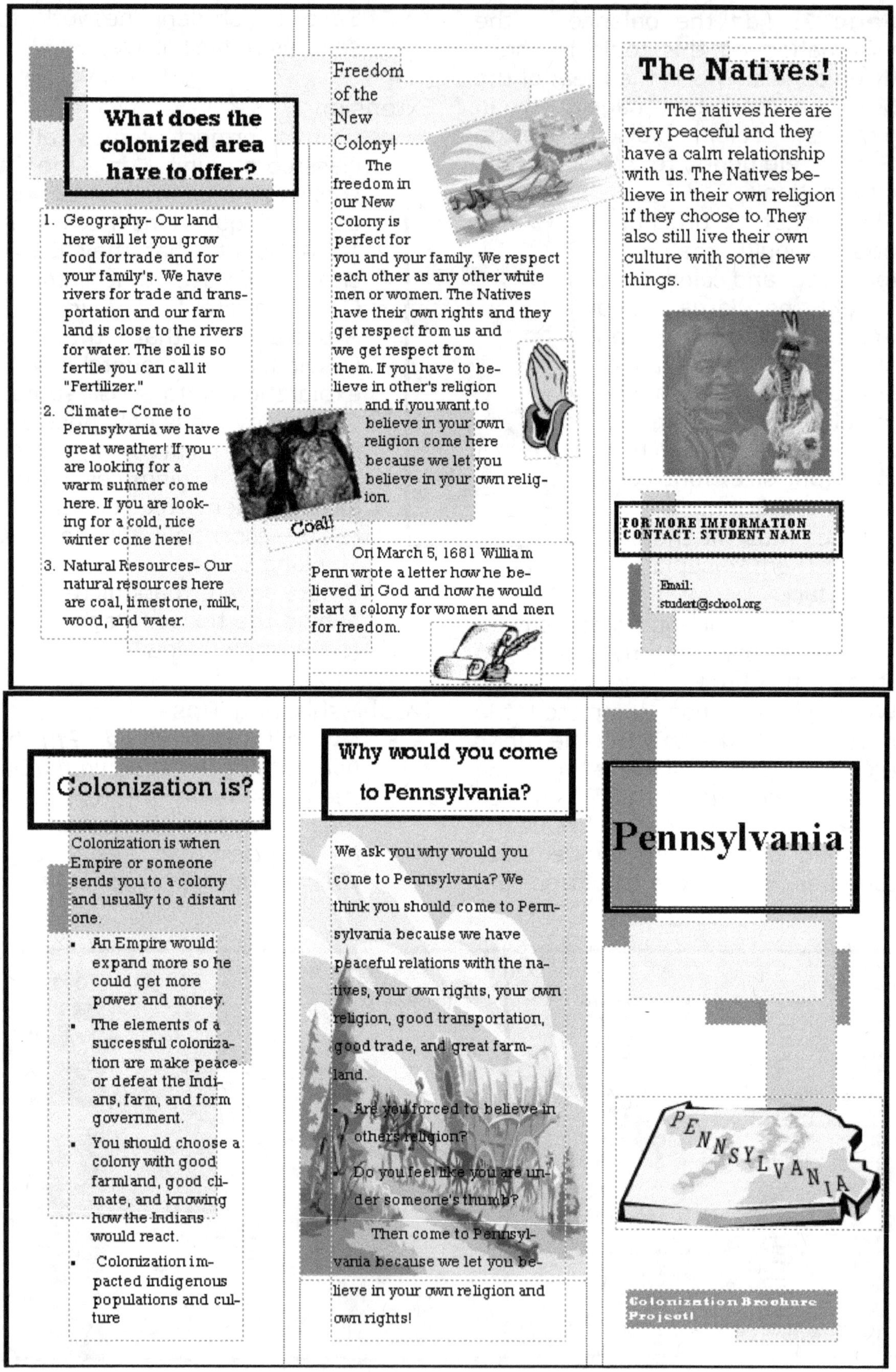

What does the colonized area have to offer?

1. Geography- Our land here will let you grow food for trade and for your family's. We have rivers for trade and transportation and our farm land is close to the rivers for water. The soil is so fertile you can call it "Fertilizer."
2. Climate– Come to Pennsylvania we have great weather! If you are looking for a warm summer come here. If you are looking for a cold, nice winter come here!
3. Natural Resources- Our natural resources here are coal, limestone, milk, wood, and water.

Coal!

Freedom of the New Colony!

The freedom in our New Colony is perfect for you and your family. We respect each other as any other white men or women. The Natives have their own rights and they get respect from us and we get respect from them. If you have to believe in other's religion and if you want to believe in your own religion come here because we let you believe in your own religion.

On March 5, 1681 William Penn wrote a letter how he believed in God and how he would start a colony for women and men for freedom.

The Natives!

The natives here are very peaceful and they have a calm relationship with us. The Natives believe in their own religion if they choose to. They also still live their own culture with some new things.

FOR MORE INFORMATION CONTACT: STUDENT NAME

Email: student@school.org

Colonization is?

Colonization is when Empire or someone sends you to a colony and usually to a distant one.

- An Empire would expand more so he could get more power and money.
- The elements of a successful colonization are make peace or defeat the Indians, farm, and form government.
- You should choose a colony with good farmland, good climate, and knowing how the Indians would react.
- Colonization impacted indigenous populations and culture

Why would you come to Pennsylvania?

We ask you why would you come to Pennsylvania? We think you should come to Pennsylvania because we have peaceful relations with the natives, your own rights, your own religion, good transportation, good trade, and great farmland.

- Are you forced to believe in others religion?
- Do you feel like you are under someone's thumb?

Then come to Pennsylvania because we let you believe in your own religion and own rights!

Pennsylvania

PENNSYLVANIA

Colonization Brochure Project!

Trifold Brochure—Advanced
Grading Rubric

Your name: ______________________________

Your homeroom teacher: ______________________

1. Title Page **4 points**

a. *Eye catching and clear* ________
b. *All fonts match* ________
c. *Brochure title stands out* ________
d. *Your name and class in smaller font* ________
e. *White space filled* ________
f. *Grammar and spelling* ________

2. Back page **4 points**

a. *Eye catching and clear* ________
b. *All fonts match* ________
c. *Picture and text fill white space* ________
d. *Heading in larger font* ________
e. *Grammar and spelling* ________

3. Inside **9 points**

a. *Headings in larger font* ________
b. *All fonts match* ________
c. *No white spaces* ________
d. *Pictures fit events discussed* ________
e. *Spell-check* ________
f. *Grammar check* ________

4. Overall Professional Look **3 points**

(inside print lines, attractive look, organized, easy to understand, etc.)

How I grade myself: ______________________________

Explain: ______________________________

Subject #4: History

Project #54: Sponge Activities in History. Six edutainment websites to be visited in spare time in the classroom (as with all sponges). Each deals with history and can be enjoyed with only a few minutes of time

Higher-order thinking skills	Technology-specific:	Subject Area/ Learning-specific	Standard: ISTE
Applying—use concepts in new situations	*Use technology to broaden subject matter competency, learn the basics of internet*	*Reinforce spelling, class word lists*	*3b, 3c*

Grade level: 2-8
Prior knowledge: Project 99: Internet Basx (if you have Book II of this collection)
Time required: 5-10 minutes
Software required: internet
Vocabulary: Sponge, Ctrl+click, address bar, website address

Lesson Description

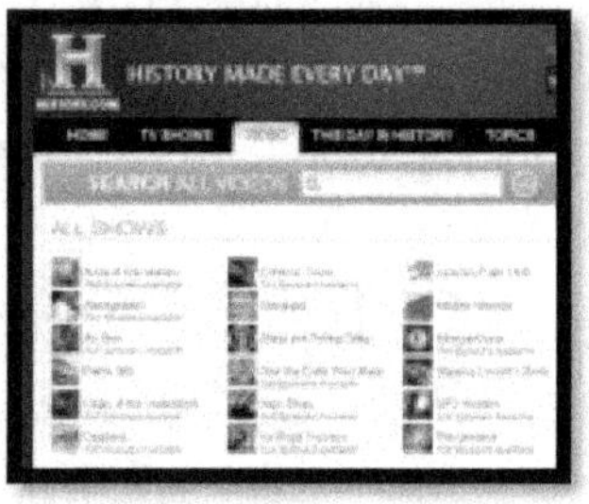

- What's a sponge activity? The term was originally coined and used by Madeline Hunter. A "sponge" is an activity designed to produce learning during the times taken up by "administrivia." These sponges stem from Hunter's teaching philosophy that there should be no wasted moments in her classroom.
- Each of these websites offers quick activities for students, taking 5-10 minutes.
- Ctrl+click on the blue links to take you to the site

Computer Activity

- History Happens: Stories on Video
- Newspaper front pages from around the world—interactiv
- When they were Young: A Photographic History of Children
- Road to Revolution Game
- Playing History--games on all sorts of historic topics; may be young for HS or perfect

Extensions

- Add the websites to favorites to be used more quickly
- If you purchased a digital copy of this text, click the images to reach the website

Troubleshooting Tips

- *When I type the address, I get a list of hits. (Did you type the address into the search bar, not the address bar?)*
- *I can't find the site you're talking about, but I'm on the page (take a deep breath, read some of the information on the page and it'll get you there. Don't worry: You're going to have fun!)*

Subject #5: Keyboarding

Project #55: Keyboarding in the Classroom. Mix a variety of keyboarding tools so students get the most out of typing time in the classroom. I include software (TTL4), online keyboarding websites (Type Dojo) and fun tests (TypingTest). The goal is to get students to age-appropriate national standards for typing speed with just two-three times per week, fifteen minutes each time.

Higher-order thinking skills	Technology-specific:	Subject Area/ Learning-specific	Standard: ISTE
Analyze (see patterns) *Knowledge (master material)*	*Understand and use technology systems*	*Speed and accuracy, posture, good habits*	*1d*

Grade level: K-8
Prior knowledge: Computer basics
Time required: 15 minutes, two-three times a week
Software required: Class typing program
Vocabulary: home row, posture

Lesson Description

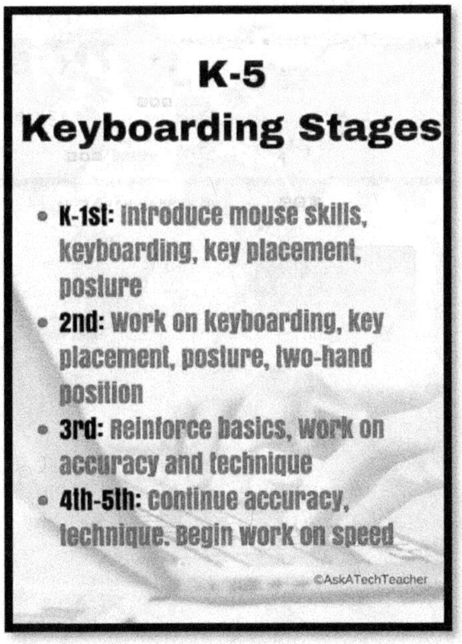

- Like all sports, typing honors speed and accuracy, and gets better with practice. But, it's human nature to stop trying when we get bored. This lesson addresses keyboarding boredom.
- Of all technology skills students learn, keyboarding is arguably the most important. The better they are at it, the easier is schoolwork and the less resistant they are to completing it.
- This lesson, with Project 56 and 57 (from Book II of this collection) provides a three-pronged attack against weak keyboarding skills.

Computer Activity

- **Phase one:** For K, 1—beginning readers and prekeyboarders—focus on using a keyboard with two hands, one on each side. Don't worry about finger placement, speed or accuracy. Good starting programs are Brown Bear Typing and Type to Learn Jr.
  - TTL Jr. (and some others) divides keys by red for left hand and blue for right. I put the same color dot on the children's hands, to remind them which to use for which key.
  - Within 18 months, move them up to a full-fledged program that teaches finger placement and starts thinking about speed and accuracy.
- Many programs that serve this need (Type to Learn, Typing Club, or Typing Web for example) allow teachers to track progress by using the administrator account to set words per minute and accuracy goals. Make sure students log in to take advantage of this feature.
- **Phase two:** As soon as the focus moves from hands-on-keyboard to

fingers-on-keyboard, students must develop good habits: Hands curled over home row, each to its own side. Stretch for keys at the top and bottom. Good posture. Keep eyes on the screen.

- Students move forward at their own pace. Remind them to pay attention to instructions and don't worry about speed—that'll come.

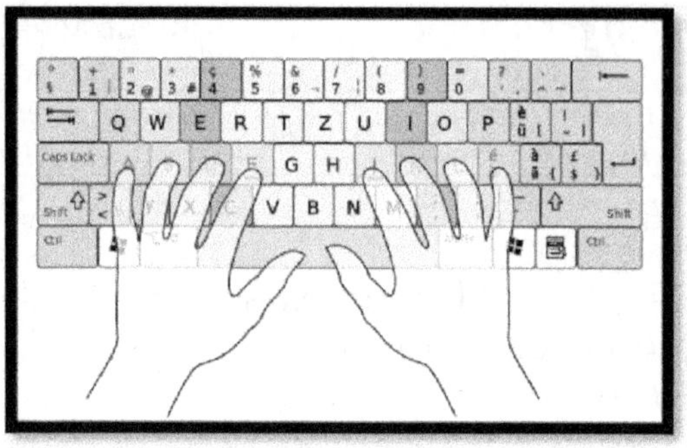

- When the student finishes the program, either start over (if it's a new year) or graduate them to *All the Right Type* or another regulated keyboarding program (for variety)
- **Phase three:** Good habits in place, students now focus on touch typing, speed and accuracy. This takes them through to the end of organized training.

Extensions

- Have students use online typing programs occasionally. The variety will sharpen their skills.

Troubleshooting Tips

- *I can't get past this Lesson. (You're promoted when you hit the mandated speed and accuracy level).*

KEYBOARDING HINTS

These came directly from the classroom, tested on 400 students a year. These are the most common fixes that help students excel at keyboarding:

1. **Tuck elbows against the sides of your body. This keeps hands in the right spot—home row**
2. **Use your RIGHT thumb for the space bar. That leaves hands on home row**
3. **Curl fingers over home row—they're cat paws, not dog paws**
4. **Use inside fingers for inside keys, outside fingers for outside keys**
5. **Use the finger closest to the key you need. Sounds simple, but this isn't what usually happens with beginners.**
6. **Keep pointers anchored to *f* and *j***
7. **Play keyboard like a piano (or violin, or guitar, or recorder). You'd never use your pointer for all keys**
8. **Fingers move, not your hands. Hands stay anchored to the *f* and *j* keys**
9. **Don't use caps lock for capitals! Use shift.**
10. **Add a barrier between sides of the keyboards. I fashioned one from cover stock. That'll remind students to stay on the correct side of keyboard**

Assume the Position

- Legs centered in front of body
- Elbows at sides
- Body centered in front of keyboard
- Hands curved over home row
- Document to left of computer
- Use right thumb for space bar
- Eyes on screen

Index

Thanks for purchasing!
Terms of Use
according to American Copyright Laws
DO...
• Use this item for personal use, your class, your students
• Review/share your experiences online provided you link back to the AATT store
• Buy additional licenses
DON'T...
• Copy, email, or post to a shared account
• Post this item or a portion (> 10%) be it to your website, school server, another
• Share it, sell, claim it as your own
• Use any part of this to create another product for sharing, selling
Please visit me!
BL
OG

www.ingramcontent.com/pod-product-compliance
Lightning Source LLC
LaVergne TN
LVHW060547061126
851857LV00017B/1923